BRIGHT NOTES

STEPPENWOLF BY HERMANN HESSE

Intelligent Education

Nashville, Tennessee

BRIGHT NOTES: Steppenwolf
www.BrightNotes.com

No part of this publication may be used or reproduced in any manner whatsoever without written permission, except in the case of brief quotations in critical articles and reviews. For permissions, contact Influence Publishers http://www.influencepublishers.com.

ISBN: 978-1-645422-18-1 (Paperback)
ISBN: 978-1-645422-19-8 (eBook)

Published in accordance with the U.S. Copyright Office Orphan Works and Mass Digitization report of the register of copyrights, June 2015.

Originally published by Monarch Press.
John D. Simons, 1972
2020 Edition published by Influence Publishers.

Interior design by Lapiz Digital Services. Cover Design by Thinkpen Designs.

Printed in the United States of America.

Library of Congress Cataloging-in-Publication Data forthcoming.
Names: Intelligent Education
Title: BRIGHT NOTES: Steppenwolf
Subject: STU004000 STUDY AIDS / Book Notes

CONTENTS

1) Introduction to Hermann Hesse — 1

2) Interpretation and Analysis of Steppenwolf — 18

3) Characterization In Steppenwolf — 69

4) Chronological Table Of Hesse's Main Works — 78

5) Essay Questions And Answers — 80

6) Annotated Bibliography — 89

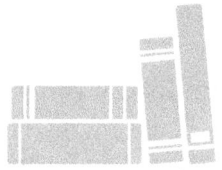

INTRODUCTION TO HERMANN HESSE

FAMILY BACKGROUND

Like many German writers, Hermann Hesse came from a family which had for many generations been associated with the Protestant clergy. The father, Johannes Hesse, was a protestant clergyman who belonged to the pietistic tradition, a liberal branch of German Protestantism which stressed a concern for the individual's relationship to God above strict formal dogma. Hermann was later to acknowledge the importance of the religious atmosphere of his childhood, as, for example, in a letter dated 1950 in which he spoke of Christianity as it was lived, rather than preached, in his home. Johannes Hesse spent the years 1869 to 1873 as a missionary in India. There he acquired an interest in Oriental philosophy and theology which he was to retain for the rest of his life. Forced to return to Europe on account of poor health, he settled in Calw, a town in Southwestern Germany, where he was active as an author of works on religious subjects. Hermann's mother, Marie, came from a similar background; she had been in India as the wife of a missionary. She was living in Calw after the death of her first husband when she met Johannes Hesse.

Hermann, the second of six children, was born in Calw on July 2nd 1877. Four years later the family moved to Basel,

Switzerland, and acquired Swiss citizenship. The father continued his religious work in Basel where he became the editor of a missionary magazine. In 1886 the family returned to Calw where Hesse was to remain until leaving home to attend a boarding school in 1890. Hermann's early childhood years were for the most part pleasant and they were certainly intellectually stimulating. Literature, philosophy, and the arts were discussed and respected in his home. Guests, many of whom came from foreign lands, were often entertained there. Hermann felt an especial affinity to his mother whose loving care provided him with a feeling of security and well-being. His father, on the other hand, in spite of his tolerance in regard to many theological matters, believed in strict discipline and followed rigid theories of education which allowed no room for freedom of expression on his son's part. Many of the difficulties of these early years are reflected in Hesse's works, as, for example, in "A Child's Heart." As a boy, Hermann was not an outstanding pupil and did not enjoy school; he once remarked that he had had only one teacher whom he admired.

SEARCH FOR A CAREER

As was common in Germany at that time, Hermann was sent to a boarding school to prepare for the difficult examination which all students had to pass in order to be admitted to advanced schools and the university. He entered the school in Göppingen in 1890 to undertake this preparation. At this school, for the only time in his life, he was an exceptionally good student. After successfully passing the examination, he followed the wishes of his father and enrolled in the famous school at Maulbronn with the intention of becoming a Protestant minister. The atmosphere of the school soon proved too oppressive and Hermann ran away. He returned, but once more was unable to adjust and soon left the school permanently. The months which followed were exceedingly traumatic for the disturbed youth. Help was sought from various persons and institutions, but Hermann's emotional problems could not be alleviated. Once he even went so far as to attempt suicide. His final exposure to formal education was at a preparatory school in Bad Cannstatt in 1893 and 1894. Hesse was not at all happy there and his experiences formed the basis for the descriptions of some of Sinclair's unhappy school experiences in *Demian*.

While doing mechanical work in a Calw clock factory in 1894 and 1895, the young Hesse decided that he wanted to become a writer. He soon found employment in a bookstore in Tübingen and began to see meaning, or at least potential meaning, in life. In 1899 he published his first books, a collection of poetry and one of short prose pieces. In that same year he moved to Basel where he continued to work in the book trade and to expand his horizons, by reading books of many different kinds, and by traveling in Switzerland and Italy. Two years later he wrote a book which attracted the attention of some important German critics and which accordingly established Hesse's reputation as an author: *The Posthumous Papers and Poems of Hermann Lauscher*.

IMPORTANT EARLY WRITINGS

Other books followed, including, in 1904, the novel *Peter Camenzind*. This book was immediately successful and the royalties from it and from other writings gave Hesse a degree of financial independence. He was accordingly able to leave the book trade and devote himself entirely to his writing. The novel is about a poor but talented Swiss boy who grows up in harmony with nature, but decides to go out into the world where he eventually attains a measure of material success in society. He ultimately comes to realize that he has not found self-fulfillment in love, intellectual pursuits, art, music, or material goods. Following the death of his close friend Boppi, a cripple, he finally retires to lead an isolated life free of the demands of society. Already in the first of Hesse's novels we see very clearly the **theme** that will pervade all of the later ones: the difficult search on the part of an individual for identity and fulfillment.

Hesse soon became a respected member of the German literary elite and contributed stories, poems, reviews, and essays to many of the leading periodicals of that time. He also continued to write novels and the next one, *Beneath the Wheel* (1906), was to a great extent autobiographical. It relates the unsuccessful attempt of the hero, Hans Giebenrath, to cope with the stifling atmosphere of the educational system. The two sides of Hesse's own nature are shown in Hans and in Hermann Heilner, who rebelled against the system and ran away. Hans, like Hesse, experienced many disappointments and eventually found himself unable to cope with the demands of his father and of the school. In two very important respects, however, the novel does not follow Hesse's biography; Hans' mother dies when he is very young, depriving him of a source of warmth and love, and Hans himself, in a state of depression, drowns while still a young man. One of many German literary works of the early twentieth century which attacked the educational system, *Beneath the Wheel* was very popular.

Hesse's next two novels, *Gertrude* (1910) and *Rosshalde* (1914), deal with the problems of the artist. The former is one of the least autobiographical of Hesse's works. The hero, Kuhn, is a musician who enjoyed a happy childhood. He injures his leg in an accident and becomes introverted. He falls in love with Gertrude, but lacks the self-assurance to reveal his feelings to her and try to win her love. She marries another man, but the marriage is not successful and her husband commits suicide. Kuhn becomes a great composer, although he remains a lonely and unhappy person. He has limited contact with Gertrude in his later years, although she continues to be a source of inspiration for his great works of art.

YEARS OF CRISIS

In 1904 Hesse married Maria Bernoulli, a Swiss woman nine years his elder. The couple led an isolated life in Gaienhofen. Sons were born in 1905 and 1909. Hesse was a successful and highly productive writer, but his marriage became progressively less happy. In 1911 he made a journey to the Orient in the company of the painter Hans Sturzenegger. Hesse was particularly interested in India, the country in which both of his parents had lived and which his father and grandfather had studied extensively. The trip, however, did not enable Hesse to find the peace and fulfillment which he so desperately sought. Some of his impressions are recorded in *From India* (1913). His personal conflicts are reflected rather directly in the novel *Rosshalde* 1914, the story of the painter Johann Veraguth, who lives a lonely and unhappy life at his estate, Rosshalde, with his wife and a younger son, Pierre. An older son, Albert, is away at school and returns only during vacation periods. Life acquires meaning for Veraguth through his work as an artist and his love for Pierre. He tolerates his marriage only for the sake of Pierre. What remains of his happiness is shattered when Pierre dies of meningitis. The end of the novel remains open. Veraguth, turning his back on bourgeois society, leaves Rosshalde and his wife to travel. His future is uncertain.

The outbreak of World War I in 1914 marked another crisis in Hesse's complicated personal life. Although he had been living in Switzerland for many years, he was German and his reading public expected him to support the German cause. (Switzerland remained neutral during the war.) Hesse did not immediately assume an anti-German stand, but he publicly questioned the excessive patriotism in his native country which was brought out by the war and he was in turn sharply criticized from many sides in Germany. He remained in Switzerland throughout the war and was active in the effort to improve the lot of German prisoners of war and internees.

Hesse's literary productivity continued undiminished during the first years of the war and *Knulp*, one of the more popular of his earlier works, appeared in 1915. The three stories contained in the collection will be analyzed in detail in this study guide.

The following year, 1916, was to bring severe misfortune: the death of his father, the serious illness of his son Martin, and the mental breakdown of his wife, who had to be sent to an institution. This was in fact the end of Hesse's first marriage, although he did not obtain a formal divorce until 1923. Hesse was naturally despondent and his search for psychiatric help brought him in contact with Dr. Joseph Lang, a disciple of the eminent psychologist Carl Gustav Jung. From Doctor Lang, Hesse not only received advice which helped him overcome his own personal crisis, but he also learned in detail the theories of Jung. Hesse became a devoted student of Jung and the influence of this psychologist was to become one of the most important factors in his later works.

THE MIDDLE YEARS

Demian was written during a short period of time in 1917 under the immediate influence of Doctor Lang and, through him, of Jung. This new novel marks a radical break in Hesse's literary development and the author did not want his readers in any way to be reminded of his earlier works or to associate the new Hesse - the Hesse of *Demian* - with them. Accordingly he published the novel in 1919 under the pseudonym Emil Sinclair, the name of one of the main characters of the book. The novel was an immediate success. The young postwar generation felt a strong affinity to this strange, powerful work, and it was also well-received by literary critics. The Fontane Prize, a prestigious literary prize awarded for outstanding first novels, was presented to the mysterious Emil Sinclair. The prize was returned by the publisher and in 1920 Hesse revealed that he was actually the author. But he had achieved his goal. To the reading public, Hermann Hesse was now primarily known as the author of *Demian*, not of *Peter Camenzind*, *Rosshalde*, and other early works which Hesse had come to consider to be immature.

The most important **theme** of *Demian* is the necessity of first recognizing, and then integrating into one's personality, the two different aspects of life - the "light" and the "dark," the spiritual and the sensual, saintliness and sin. The setting, plot, and style of *Demian* are for the most part dissimilar from those of Hesse's previous works. It is set in Germany during the early years of the present century and describes the outer and inner development of Emil Sinclair from late childhood to maturity. Here, as in *Siddhartha*, *Narcissus and Goldmund*, and many of Hesse's works - although not in the stories discussed in this study guide - three distinct stages of development can be seen: the early period of innocence, a middle period which is not without searching, loneliness, and even despair, and the final period in which a synthesis is effected. When Emil Sinclair is first introduced to the "dark" world, he sees no way to reconcile the warm, serene atmosphere of his home with the cold frightening world he now sees. But with the help of Max Demian he gradually becomes more and more able to see the possibility of accepting both aspects of his human nature and he eventually finds he is no longer forced to view them as polar opposites.

The year 1919 was indeed an important one. Hesse wrote several important essays during that year, including "Zarathustra's Return" in which his debt to Nietzsche is acknowledged, and three of his better short stories, "A Child's Heart," "Klingsor's Last Summer" and "Klein and Wagner," published together in 1920 under the title *Klingsor's Last Summer*. These three stories will be analyzed in detail in this study guide. Furthermore, Hesse moved from Bern, where he had been living, to the small Swiss town of Montagnola, which was to be his home in his later years. It was also at about this time that Hesse first took up painting; he later became an accomplished painter and it was to remain his favorite hobby throughout his life. And finally, work on the next important book, *Siddhartha*, was begun in this year.

Siddhartha proved to be an especially difficult book to write. As Hesse remarked, the first two periods of the hero's life, those of innocence and searching, were easy for him to portray. But the final triumphant vision of the old Siddhartha was foreign to Hesse's experience and hence he had great difficulty putting it on paper. Only in 1922 was the completed novel published.

In this highly poetic book set in ancient India Hesse describes the life of Siddhartha. First the hero masters his intellect and will, and then he turns to the world of the senses. He finds neither asceticism nor hedonism totally satisfying. Late in life he finds fulfillment in a mystical vision at, and with the help of, a river, the symbol of perfection, unity, and continuity.

In 1923 Hesse became a Swiss citizen. His personal life, however, remained unsettled. He obtained a divorce from his first wife and soon thereafter (in January, 1924) he married Ruth Wenger. Five years were to lapse before the publication of his next major novel, *Steppenwolf* (1927). These years were far from totally barren. Hesse continued to publish poems, short stories, essays, and reviews in various journals and newspapers. But a feeling of alienation, which is reflected in the suffering of Harry Haller in *Steppenwolf*, continued to affect him. His second marriage, like the first, did not prove to be successful; it ended in divorce in 1927. By this time Hesse was one of the most famous writers of his generation and his first full-length biography, by Hugo Ball, appeared in conjunction with his fiftieth birthday in that same year.

Steppenwolf, like *Demian*, "Klein and Wagner," and "Klingsor's Last Summer," has a "realistic" setting in the twentieth century. The hero, Harry Haller, is a middle-aged man who is torn between the world of the bourgeoisie and that of the artist-intellectual. At first he believes that there are but two aspects of his personality, and that he is torn between these irreconcilable poles. He finds a mysterious "treatise" (reflecting insights of his own unconscious) which points out that his conception of a simple duality within himself was incorrect. There are not two Harry Hallers, the Steppenwolf and the bourgeois citizen, but many very different aspects of a complicated individual. Haller gradually comes to realize and accept this fact on a conscious level during the remainder of the novel, and the closing scene, the so-called "Magic Theater," symbolically represents the progress which he has made.

In 1930 one of Hesse's most popular novels appeared, *Narcissus and Goldmund*. Set in the Middle Ages (although not in any specific century), with a plot rich in adventure, the novel examines the duality of spirit and nature, incorporated by the two leading characters, Narcissus and Goldmund, respectively. Most of the story is devoted to Goldmund's wanderings. Originally a seminarian, he is told by his friend and teacher Narcissus that he is not destined for the priesthood. He leaves the seminary and has many adventures. He has brief, but meaningful, affairs with many women; he experiences birth and death, and is himself forced to kill another human being; and great effort he becomes a skilled sculptor and produces a few pieces of extraordinary beauty. Narcissus, on the other hand, becomes a priest and intellectual. Each respects the other, and Narcissus often helps his friend in one way or another. Although Goldmund dies a realistic and un-idealized death, his way of life, which includes both the spirit and the senses, is presented as superior to that of Narcissus, whose philosophy attempts to deny death, and who, as a result, will not be able to face death when it comes, as it inevitably must. In many respects this novel invites comparison with *Knulp*.

Hesse married again in 1931. His third wife, with whom he was to remain until his death some thirty years later, was Ninon Auslander Dolbin. Hesse's happiness during these years is portrayed symbolically in the highly autobiographical, but equally unrealistic, novel *Journey to the East* (1932). The hero is named "H.H.," an obvious **allusion** to Hermann Hesse, and many other references to the author's life can be detected in the book. Once again the hero goes through three stages in his development. He naively and confidently joins a secret Order or League and takes part in its "Journey to the East." He later drops out of the League and experiences intense loneliness and despair. With the help of Andreas Leo, a figure who resembles the old Siddhartha in some respects, he finally comes to understand the League, and himself, and then comes to feel a sense of harmony with the world.

For Hesse, unlike most important German-speaking writers, Hitler's rise to power in the early 1930s did not signal any radical changes. Hesse was already a Swiss citizen and although his hatred of war - and of the other things for which Nazism stood-remained undiminished, he was not and never had been a political activist. He had little faith in practical politics and hence did not join the active political opposition to the Nazis. In the early 1930s, under the dark cloud which covered Europe, Hesse began work on his last great novel, *The Glass Bead Game*, or *Magister Ludi*, as it is often called in English. According to Hesse's original plans, this work was to consist of a number of "autobiographies" which would describe successive reincarnations of a single person. Hesse's conception of the novel changed as he was writing it and the emphasis shifted to the final historical period, the world of Castalia, about the year 2400 A.D. The three autobiographies of Joseph Knecht that are appended to the novel are vestiges of the original plan, and a fourth autobiography was also written but not included in the book. As Hesse himself later stated, the writing of *The Glass Bead Game* was his own spiritual defense against the deadly political and moral climate in the world at that time.

Joseph Knecht's biographies and poems, which are appended to the narrator's dry, pedantic biography, most clearly reveal the novel's important issues and themes. Knecht comes to realize that he must seek oneness with nature, but is not able to formulate his ideas, let alone express them adequately and directly in words. He ultimately does realize that he cannot find what he is seeking in the rarified atmosphere of Castalia, and accordingly forsakes it in favor of a life in the "real" world. He dies before coming to a full conscious realization of the significance of his feelings and actions, and critics hence sometimes debate the validity of his life. But he has remained true to himself, and his life must therefore be called successful.

OLD AGE

Hesse's reputation continued to grow after the publication of *The Glass Bead Game*. He was awarded the Nobel Prize for literature - the world's highest literary award-in 1946, and later received several other important prizes and awards in recognition of his literary work. He continued to write poetry and short prose pieces and he faithfully answered the numerous letters addressed to him by admiring readers, although he felt uncomfortable in the role of advisor and father confessor. But *The Glass Bead Game* was to be his last novel. As the years went by, he guarded his privacy more and more carefully and seldom left his secluded home at Montagnola, of which he was so fond. He died of a brain hemorrhage on August 9, 1962, a month after his eighty-fifth birthday.

INTELLECTUAL INFLUENCES

It would be impossible even to list all of the important influences on Hesse. He was exposed to theology, philosophy, literature, and the other arts at an early age and retained his varied interests throughout his long life. Among the literary figures whom he most admired, however, two deserve particular mention: the mystical Romantic poet Novalis (pseudonym of Friedrich von Hardenberg, 1772-1801), and Johann Wolfgang von Goethe (1749-1832), about whom Hesse once said: "Among all German writers, Goethe is the one to whom I owe the most, the one to whom I am most deeply indebted, who has held my attention, enslaved and encouraged me, forced me to follow his lead or vigorously attack it." Hesse also knew many religious and philosophical writers. As was mentioned above, Christianity was quite important as a formative influence. He also studied various Eastern religions in some depth.

Two of the most important influences on Hesse's thought must be discussed here: the philosopher and poet Friedrich Nietzsche (1844-1900) and the psychologist Carl Gustav Jung (1875-1961). Before going into the extent of these influences, however, it must be emphasized that individuality remained one of Hesse's fundamental values. He read Nietzsche and Jung, as well as Goethe, Novalis, Dostoevski, Freud, and other great writers, but always with a critical eye. Although Hesse did not imitate Nietzsche, Jung, or anyone else, an understanding of certain basic concepts of Nietzsche and Jung can facilitate the approach to some of Hesse's difficult works.

Nietzsche and Jung share some important beliefs which are also to be found in the works of Hesse. Perhaps the most important of these is the insistence upon the necessity of finding one's own path toward self-realization, and of accepting the dark, so-called "sinful" side of human nature in the process. Nietzsche called for a complete revaluation of moral standards entirely eliminating the Judeo-Christian morality which he felt represented a philosophy that valued weakness and conformity rather than strength and individuality, which be preferred. Hesse, too, continually rejects weakness and conformity. The concept which Nietzsche called amor fati ("Love of fate") is likewise shared by Hesse. This concept refers to a joyful acceptance of the world as it is; it is a highly affirmative philosophy, and variations of it can be seen in Klingsor and Klein.

Jung, in more practical terms, refers to the inferior, animalistic side of our nature as the "shadow," and warns against the bad effects of simply attempting to repress it. This part of our human nature must rather be first understood, and then accepted, he maintains. Other of Jung's concepts are also useful in understanding Hesse, especially those of the "unconscious" and the "archetype." Jung believes that a large body of experiences remain in a person's unconscious (he objects to Freud's term "subconscious," which seems to him to carry derogatory implications). Each individual has elements which are part of his "personal unconscious"; that is, memories and emotions from his past which have been removed from his immediate conscious memory, but which may still exert an important and even decisive effect on his behavior unconsciously. There are also elements of the unconscious which are shared by everyone. Jung studied ancient symbols and myths, and analyzed the dreams of his contemporaries. He came to the conclusion that many symbols recur even though modern man may not have known of the ancient representations. Such symbols which have universal significance are said by Jung to be part of the "collective unconscious," and are called "archetypes."

Finally, Jung coined the term "anima" to refer to an unconscious feminine aspect within a man through which he can to some extent intuitively comprehend the nature of women. The references in *Demian* to masculine traits in a woman, or feminine traits in a man, are based on this concept, and many apparent **allusions** to homosexuality, which some critics are fond of pointing out, can likewise be explained on the basis of Jung's concept. The several aspects of personality, in Jung's formulation, must be integrated if a person, man or woman, is to attain fulfillment. They must accordingly always be considered as parts of a whole, and not as isolated components.

HESSE'S POPULARITY

The history of Hesse's popularity in Germany and America is complex and, on the surface at least, enigmatic. He was a competent popular novelist and essayist during the first two decades of this century and enjoyed a certain following among the German reading public at that time. Upon the publication of *Demian* in 1919, he immediately became one of the heroes of one segment of the younger generation in Germany. His disillusionment with the war and his visionary, even mystical attitude toward the future contributed greatly to his popularity and to his success (although it should be noted that some Germans reproached him for his lack of patriotism during the war). His popularity in German-speaking countries remained high until the early 1930s, when Hitler assumed power in Germany. Because they were largely unpolitical, Hesse's books were not immediately burned and banned in Germany, but his work was not encouraged or even approved by the Nazi hierarchy. Many important intellectuals and writers, both German and non-German, praised Hesse highly. Among these are T.S. Elliot, André Gide, and Thomas Mann. After a brief period of popularity in Europe following the Second World War, Hesse's reputation began to decline, both among academicians and the younger generation of readers. At the present time, Hesse's reputation in Germany is at an all-time low. The young radicals, especially, have no use for his writings since they associate them with the Romantic past - including Nazism! - which they desire to overcome and leave behind.

Hesse has been widely translated into non-European languages, and his reception in India and Japan, especially, has been consistently favorable, and not subject to the ups and downs which mark his popularity in Germany and in America. Hesse was proud of the fact that readers in Eastern countries appreciated his works, which contain many elements of Eastern philosophy.

The history of Hesse's reception in America is quite different from that of his reception in Germany. Although several of his works had appeared in translation throughout the years, he was all but unknown in this country when he received the Nobel Prize for Literature in 1946. The American press for the most part ignored him, even when he received this prestigious award. It was only in the late 1950s that Americans began to become interested in his work. Today, of course, he has become a cult figure. Hesse is without doubt one of the very favorite authors of college-age Americans. Similarly, most of the serious scholarly criticism on Hesse in recent years has been written in English, and most of the important books have been written by North Americans.

It is certainly easy to see why American youth is interested in Hesse. The problems with which he deals in his stories and novels have meaning for young people in this country today. His treatment of adolescence, the problems of growing up, authority, rebellion, the "establishment," sex, human relationships, and, to a lesser extent, drugs, is significant and "relevant." Likewise, many young people share Hesse's interest in Oriental philosophy and in a non-dogmatic theology. It must, however, be pointed out that many important elements of Hesse's thought are overlooked by the majority of his admirers. For example, one often sees a devotion to self-discipline and hard work directed toward the achievement of some specific goal in Hesse's work. Especially Demian, Siddhartha, and Joseph Knecht attain a remarkable amount of self-discipline while still quite young, and it becomes clear in the respective works that the success and happiness of these characters is possible only because of their earlier rigorous training. If Hesse does not share the Protestant ethic of hard work, he nonetheless sees and portrays in his novels the necessity of building one's life on a firm foundation. Many of his works also show the other side of the coin - the results of not building one's life on a firm foundation (e.g., Klein and Knulp, who is much less happy than the more disciplined wanderer Goldmund). Hesse in no way respects bourgeois narrow-mindedness, complacency, and resistance to change at all cost; but neither does he express approval of destructive rebellion for its own sake. The freedom of Hesse's characters is a reflection of a successful, integrated life; they are slaves neither to tradition nor to their own weaknesses.

It is especially ironic that Hesse has become a folk hero and a model for an entire generation, for Hesse's most important **theme** throughout his mature works is the necessity of each individual finding his own way in life, rather than following the doctrine or teachings of an authority-figure, however noble or admirable such a figure may be. Often the incidentals of Hesse's novels and stories-rebellion against authority, sexual freedom, etc. - are religiously praised and faithfully followed by his young readers, who thereby completely lose touch with the fundamental aspect of Hesse's thought: the value of an individual's determining, choosing, and continually reexamining his own values. Surely nothing is more foreign to Hesse than the idea that "I have found the way, and there is no other." And this is indeed the narrow-minded philosophy of some of those who have chosen Hesse as their hero and mentor.

It is difficult to predict what direction Hesse's future popularity will take. More and more of his works are being translated into English - short stories, essays on various subjects, poems, autobiographical sketches, indeed almost anything will be eagerly purchased by his faithful reading public. Sooner or later a reaction must take place. Much of Hesse's short prose fiction is not especially rich or rewarding; his essays are to a great extent dated and have only historical interest; his range as a poet is narrow and poetry is in any event difficult to translate, or to appreciate in translation; and his autobiographical works are unquestionably among his least successful. It is to be hoped that these minor works will enable the American reader to more fully appreciate the complexity of Hesse, without detracting from his truly great novels and short stories.

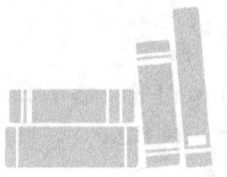

STEPPENWOLF

INTERPRETATION AND ANALYSIS

NOTE TO THE STUDENT

This study guide is intended to help you in your appreciation and evaluation of Hermann Hesse's *Steppenwolf*. It is intended as an in-depth study-guide to - and not a substitute for - the original literary work. Most of the discussion will make sense to you only if you are already familiar with the novel itself (published in English translation by Holt, Rinehart, and Winston, Inc.). This critical commentary is offered with the assumption that it will prompt you to refer back to the original text. A bibliography of Hesse's works will be found at the end of this guide, together with an annotated bibliography of selected critical works.

INTERPRETATION AND ANALYSIS OF STEPPENWOLF

Preface

We are introduced to the story of Harry Haller through the Preface. The unnamed writer is the nephew of Harry's landlady. We learn that his arrival in the house took place several years before the writing of the Preface and that he lived there for about ten months. During the last few weeks of his stay, the new lodger apparently underwent an extraordinary change both inwardly and outwardly. Suddenly he disappeared without a word, leaving behind a manuscript which the narrator decides to publish as an example of the modern intellect in despair.

The narrator's description of Harry Haller permits us to view him from the perspective of an average middle-class citizen. He tells us that Harry offended his sensibilities and that even today he feels uneasy in the knowledge that such men exist. The nephew seems well aware of the reasons behind his impulsive first dislike of Harry. Although both he and his aunt later grow quite fond of Harry, they sense that Harry is ill, not physically, but in the spirit or character. They instinctively recoil at the spectacle of a man dying inwardly. As we learn later, Harry's sickness consists of a frightening self-contempt and a lack of harmony among his many powers. This inner disharmony is externally manifested in his irregular eating and sleeping habits, excessive drinking, and the artistic disorder of his rooms. Even his reading matter is revealing: Goethe, Novalis, and Dostoevsky. Later in the novel, we understand why Harry empathizes with these writers' often agonizing efforts to find meaning in human existence and to create new values for an age that has lost its way.

The source of Harry's sickness lies in his particular upbringing. Harry was taught that certain thoughts were despicable in themselves. It followed that he ended by regarding himself in the same way. As a child he was too strong and resilient to be broken and was intelligent enough to see that his "sinful" thoughts were a product of his own mind and not the workings of some diabolical evil force. So it comes as no surprise that however viciously the mature Harry attacks institutions and persons, he never excludes himself. Try as he might to love his fellow men, he finds it impossible. His whole life demonstrates that one cannot love one's neighbor without first loving oneself.

It is precisely this loneliness and suffering that most impress the narrator and attract him to Harry. It is also the cause of this suffering which Harry had once discussed with him that leads the nephew to publish Harry's notes. For in the history of civilization, one age usually spends itself before the following one begins, thus providing for a smooth transition. Conflicts between the particular views of religion and ethics are minimized. Occasionally, as in the period following World War I, a new age begins while the old one is still vigorous. The generation caught between the two, finding it impossible simply to declare for one or the other, loses all feeling for values, morality, and security. The continual effort to create some personal order from this chaos reduces life to hell.

Harry Haller's Notes

For Madmen Only: The English title of the section "For Madmen Only" is misleading. The German equivalent for madmen - Verrückte - loses its intended ambiguous meaning in translation. According to the context, it may signify either "insane" or "madmen," or it may also mean "displaced." The latter **connotation** more accurately applies to Harry, for as the story develops, it becomes apparent that he is not just a "madman" but one who is out of step with society, or dis-placed.

Harry's displaced relationship to both himself and to life is underscored from the outset. Harry's physical discomforts are more often than not accompanied by a sensation of inner emptiness brought on by the daily ritual of witnessing man's inhuman treatment of his fellow creatures. He is grieved that men have managed civilization so badly, that they have been unable or unwilling to live according to the noble ideals which their best minds and even their religions have conceived. The materialistic system of values, the rapacious hedonism, and worst of all, the callous indifference to widespread suffering, all contribute to create in men like Harry a boundless contempt for humanity.

It is Harry's fate that he is unable to come to terms with a civilization that glorifies generals, sports heroes, and the Hit Parade, while consigning the best that man has produced in literature and the arts to the limbo of library basements and museums. The vast majority of men vilify the educated and are suspicious of anyone whose intelligence exceeds the average. The average man seeks to live a contented existence devoid of extreme pleasure or extreme anguish, an existence in which the days follow one another in dreary sameness, much like the day Harry has just spent.

The reader is surprised that it is precisely such emotional contentment that fills Harry with loathing. Not for society but for himself. His hatred of the bourgeois class is so intense that when he observes the slightest similarity between it and himself he is immediately nauseated. Comfort and satisfaction upset him so much that in desperation he annihilates his tranquility by whatever means are at hand. He prefers even the most infernal torture to the soothing oblivion of an emotionless existence.

Thus Harry's rebellion against the bourgeois ideal of an even-heated, passionless existence amounts to an attack against the bourgeois elements still remaining within him. It is a self-disgust born of the realization that there dwells in him much of the bourgeois longing for security and contentment. His rebellion, therefore, is as much a desperate effort to assert his independence as to assure himself that he is free of the bourgeois standard. Yet as the story unfolds, we see that his independence is an illusion and that the chief source of his unhappiness lies in his paradoxical, love-hate relationship to that class. Even though he despises the bourgeois way of life, he chooses to live in middle-class houses that are spotlessly clean, smelling of soap and furniture polish. Although he keeps his own rooms in disorder, he likes the atmosphere of a quiet and respectable existence around him. In fact, Harry's paradoxical admiration of the bourgeois has all the outward signs of religion. He treats the small vestibule on the second floor landing as a temple where he often stops. Carrying the religious symbolism further, he meditates upon the two potted plants there with his hands folded as in prayer. Behind the temple he imagines an inner sanctum full of symbolic religious paraphernalia.

The Steel Helmet: As might be expected, Harry's nocturnal hangout is not frequented by artists, authors, and other outsiders, but is the gathering place of ordinary people who sip their wine in stolid silence. The tavern is another of Harry's temples of respectability. There he can sit at sturdy wooden tables and drink wine from thick peasant glasses.

Harry persists in attaching no significance to his preference for middle-class surroundings. He tells himself that he has nothing in common with that world; he is merely succumbing to an old sentimentality. By this time the reader has already begun to suspect that there is something terribly wrong with Harry. For instance, what about his intellectual honesty if in one breath he rails at the bourgeois and in the next expresses his fondness for it? And again, how is it possible for someone who obviously possesses a keen and intelligent mind to blithely ignore a situation that approaches hypocrisy? For an answer to this question we must wait until later. To anticipate, the answer is revealed in "The Treatise on the Steppenwolf" which now falls into his hands in a very peculiar way.

The Neon Sign And The Placard Bearer: Returning home that same evening, he encounters a weary placard-bearer who shoves some printed matter in his hands. At home he discovers the booklet "Treatise on the Steppenwolf. Not for Everybody."

The experience with the placard-bearer and the mysterious flickering sign above the portal is not an excursion into the fantastic or the supernatural for everything that subsequently happens to Harry takes place on two levels: The level of ordinary reality and the symbolical, surrealistic level created by his own mind.

As the novel progresses, Hesse gradually interweaves the surreal with the real so that in the Magic Theater they merge into one. The author brings about the illusion of the fantastic by using a technical device familiar to every student of German Romanticism. First, the fantastic vision is always constructed of material gathered from reality. The mind's metaphysical translation of everyday events is then presented as if they were real in the usual sense of the word. Through the constant juxtaposition of the real and the imaginary, the illusion of the fantastic is created. Thus, the fantastic elements in *Steppenwolf* are actually a surreal interpretation of the everyday life of modern society.

In the presentation of the hero as an extraordinary, or visionary man, we recognize yet another device of German Romanticism. A few men in every age are endowed with the capability of perceiving the miraculous in mundane reality. This facility, however, is reserved for the elect, for those of poetic spirit, for madmen. Harry is one of those rare individuals capable of creating in his mind **imagery** whose intensity equals that of concrete reality. For such persons, illusion and reality are no longer polar opposites but are fused into one.

In the light of the foregoing, let us now take another look at Harry's experience with the flickering sign and the placard-bearer. When he leaves his rooms angry with and disappointed in himself and the world, he is in a mood to be receptive to anything that will relieve his depression. When he sees the light cast flickering images from the wet pavement onto the wall, he interprets it as a message. Later after drinking too much wine, he encounters the worn-out placard-bearer who quickly gives him the pamphlet simply to get rid of him. But at home, Harry's overwrought mind turns it into the Treatise. In this respect it is worth recalling that the author of the Treatise reminds Harry that all the information contained therein is already known to him. If not to his conscious mind, to another, more remote mind. In terms of Jungian psychology, the Treatise's knowledge is already present in Harry's unconscious although awareness of it had been blocked by the conscious. As a result, Harry catches a glimpse into the darker regions of his mind. Finally, it should be pointed out that the Treatise as we know it is not the original but a copy - or better, translation - made for the manuscript which he leaves for the nephew. In fact, there is a hint that it is probably one of those cheap booklets sold on street corners that guarantee a more sparkling personality in one week or your money back.

TREATISE ON THE STEPPENWOLF

The Preface describes Harry from the standpoint of a typical middle-class man. In the section that follows we observe how

Harry sees himself. The author of the Treatise views Harry from a higher intelligence. Although the author of the Treatise is supposedly one of the Immortals, the reader soon realizes that it is really a more perceptive part of Harry who is speaking. In fact, the Treatise suggests this several times.

The Treatise begins by discussing a question that has plagued Harry most of his life. Why has he been unable to find contentment in his life? Because the personality of a Steppenwolf does not consist of one part but of two: human and lupine. To the human part he assigns everything that is beautiful, refined, and civilized. It is this side that is responsible for his regard for humanity and concern for its welfare. As a man he loves art, music, and literature, he experiences genuine emotion and compassion, and he longs for companionship with other men. The wolf, on the other hand, comprises that dark world of instinct and primal urges. It is an abyss of cruel and vicious impulses - wild, savage, and untamed. The Steppenwolf, then, is a combination of both man and wolf. In Harry's case, his two natures live in deadly enmity, each striving to dominate the other. Furthermore, Harry is unable to control either part and so he spends his life living now as the wolf, now as the man.

It is Harry's dual nature that is responsible for his inability to establish anything beyond superficial human relationships. Although he tells himself that he does not need human companionship, he nevertheless misses it. He longs for a friend living at the top of dark and creaky stairs whom he can surprise with a visit and sit up with through the night listening to music and talking. But his Steppenwolfian nature does not permit this. To be sure, he often knew people for a short time who were attracted to him by the part that was wolf or by the part that was man. Invariably these people deserted him when they discovered that Harry was not just wolf or just man, but a mixture of the two. Throughout his life Harry was forced to endure much unhappiness because of his inability to reconcile the conflicting elements in his soul.

Yet it happens on very rare occasions that the man and wolf make peace and work in harmony. At such times, each gives strength and inspiration to the other. Then Harry lives in a state of unequaled and sublime happiness. Furthermore, these intervals of perfect inner harmony are the periods of his most intense creative activity. It is in this inner harmony and its relationship to creative activity that the psychology of Jung is reflected. For only when such a condition exists is a man endowed with true creativity.

The Treatise points out that Harry must try to harmonize the many discordant elements in his psyche if he wishes to attain a sense of fulfillment and satisfaction as a man and as a creator. Later the Treatise shows how Harry can do this by first admitting to himself what his repressions are and then accepting them.

Freedom And Loneliness: The Treatise gives another reason for Harry's inability to come to terms with himself. Early in life he discovered that loneliness and absolute independence were essential for his productivity and joy. On this point he was firm and uncompromising. Throughout his life he sacrificed everything to preserve his independence. But what had once been his strength and source of happiness had now become a lethal curse because he found himself slowly suffocating in the vacuum of absolute loneliness that he had created for himself. Now that he no longer desired to be left alone, it had become his fate. To be sure, he often received invitations, letters, and presents from others, but no one dared come near him. Living this way in the vacuum of the lonely, cut off from human companionship, and suffering abuse from his enemies, he often contemplated suicide.

Suicide: The Treatise discusses a class of people, among them Harry Haller, who are termed suicides although they never kill themselves. Such suicides rarely stand close to death, but nevertheless, they feel themselves constantly threatened. When such people suffer a setback or an injury at the hands of society, their thoughts invariably turn to self-destruction. The reader perceives that thoughts of suicide are normal for any man who believes the point of life lies not in the discovery and perfection of the Self, but rather consists in returning to the beginning, to the primary source of being. Such people believe that the way to ultimate knowledge of God, of the All, is found in death, not in life. Fear of self-confrontation is therefore the impulse to suicide, not fear of life. In fact, without being cognizant of it, Harry manages to turn the idea of suicide into a source of strength. No matter how severe the pain, or how unsupportable the melancholy and depression, he draws comfort from the thought that if things become really unbearable the door always stands open.

Relationship To The Bourgeois: Harry is told that it is sheer hypocrisy for him to live among the bourgeois while despising it. The Treatise depicts Harry's life as a series of shabby compromises. It mocks a Harry who viciously attacks the world of finance but has money in the bank and lives off the interest; who rails at the enslavement of man by big business, yet wisely invests in the stocks of sound corporations; who likes to keep his own rooms in disorder, but always makes sure they are situated in tidy, respectable houses; who regards the fashion industry as nothing more than a collection of effete eunuchs but dresses expensively himself; and, finally, who champions the rights of the revolutionary and admires the enemy of the state and society, but always feels uncomfortable in their presence.

A premonition of his encounter with Hermine occurs when we learn that while he has no theoretical objections to prostitutes, he would be incapable of regarding one as his equal, socially or intellectually. Since Harry's life is a total contradiction, it is no wonder that despite his learning, great intelligence, and cleverness, he has been unable to find contentment with himself and with life.

It has become overly apparent that Harry suffers from an unhealthy attachment to the bourgeois. He had been raised by middle-class parents in the best middle-class tradition according to the best middle-class ethical system. Even though over the years he had succeeded in liberating himself from the basis of its ideals and beliefs, there remained a strong emotional attachment to those middle-class values of which he was unconscious. The Treatise now strips away Harry's illusions about that class.

Definition Of The Bourgeois: The term "bourbeois" as it is used throughout the novel designates a state of mind rather than an economic class. The man of bourgeois spirit seeks above all else to establish equilibrium between the countless extremes of which human nature is capable such as reason and passion, duty and inclination, nature and spirit. It is precisely between these absolutes that the bourgeois seeks his place. He refuses to abandon himself to either extreme because to do so involves some loss of identity. And since it is precisely the Self that the bourgeois wishes to preserve at all costs, he chooses to walk the middle of the road. (Hesse uses "Self" in the Jungian meaning to designate the entire psyche.) Such people strive to keep their lives like a living-room held constantly at 72 degrees. The extremes of which human nature is capable are lopped off. Anger is permitted, but not rage; love but not passion; happiness, but not ecstasy. In short, ethical absolutism is anathema and peace of mind is far preferable to the dazzling fire of total commitment. Even so such a way of life would be above all value judgments were it not for one factor. For since the bourgeois is by nature a weak and fearful creature, content with a lukewarm existence, he is easy to rule. In fact, the civilization he has created for himself reflects his weakness and insecurity. Strength, force, and self-reliance have been replaced by majority rule, law and order, and democracy.

Why The Bourgeois Prospers: Why then does the bourgeois continue to prosper if he is weak and incapable of accepting responsibility? Why do the history books recount tales of his particular kind of courage and daring, of idealism and noble self-sacrifice? Is it not true that he has created an ethic that calls for industriousness which in turn creates powerful economic systems? Does he not bring together vast armies which carry his beliefs to all parts of the globe? Is not his sense of duty, patriotism, and equality for all legendary? Do not those who are fortunate enough to dwell in his lands live the good life and enjoy material benefits and freedom that are unparalleled in the history of civilization?

The author of the Treatise says that it is not the bourgeois who should receive credit for all this, but rather the vast number of Steppenwolves like Harry who live among them. Unable to break away from bourgeois society, they are doomed to live in it and, by so doing, give it strength. Thus according to Hesse, idealism and noble self-sacrifice emanates from the Steppenwolves, from their highly developed but imprisoned individuality. In turn they loathe the ethic that puts a premium on hard work and thriftiness because in the end it merely results in knowing the price of everything and the value of nothing. Moreover, duty is an opiate preached by crafty politicians designed to spare one the onus of making a free choice between alternatives. Progress, human progress, which Hesse tells us is the only valid kind, is brought about by those wild, free, and savage natures, the Steppenwolves, who live out their lives in the icy, lonely cosmos of creative activity.

Creativity: Creativity, and thus progress, must remain an alien concept to the bourgeois because creativity implies change, and it is precisely change that is regarded with suspicion, if not hostility. The bourgeois strives to maintain the status quo, to remain static and unchanging.

Creativity and progress often rely on the unpredictable inspirational element in man that provides the necessary impulse to disobey the urge of tradition and to seek other alternatives. To discover, man must begin by upsetting moribund order and by creating disorder. Tension between tradition and order on the one hand and instability and disorder on the other is both a feature of change and a source of creativity.

If civilization is not to stagnate, it must remain in a state of eternal becoming. In a like manner Nietzsche proclaimed: "You must have chaos in yourself, if you wish to give birth to a dancing star." In each creative act man learns something of the true essence of things and in so doing transcends his former self and affirms the principle of self-improvement. In this way, men like Harry also insure the improvement of society which progresses according to the cumulative creative efforts of its individuals.

When the bourgeois denies the validity of unpredictability, change, and even chaos, they negate the mechanics by which civilizations go forward. But then the bourgeois is interested neither in progress, the individual, nor in freeing the inner man. Therefore, all that is left up to the Steppenwolves.

Humor: Such men as Harry lack that extra strength necessary to cut themselves off entirely from their roots in the bourgeois and so are doomed to live within it. They are filled with hatred for themselves because while they feel the urge to make the plunge into the untrammeled regions of the unconditional, they are unable to sustain themselves in its frigid atmosphere. Indeed, there are some men who possess enormous power and almost limitless freedom who are able to make the final leap, but they are few in number.

Since these Immortals, as Hesse calls them, prefer to be consumed by the inner fire of total commitment, their vitality and talents are lost to the bourgeois. But what of the Steppenwolves who exist between the two worlds and belong to neither? How can they live peacefully and without constant irritation in a world that is characterized by banality, triviality, and obtuseness?

The Treatise tells Harry that there is a third alternative that will at least make life bearable and productive. Humor! Here humor is not used in the ordinary sense as signifying something funny although in a way that too plays a part. It designates a specific attitude to life that is both heroic and humble. This state of mind, when properly mastered, has the power not only to reconcile all polarities but also to affirm them. This is perhaps one of the few things the Immortal lacks. For while the Immortal is capable of regarding his polar opposite as a kindred spirit, he cannot accept that middle ground between. But with humor one can do even that. Humor further signifies a kind of disengagement from life. It enables a person to live in the world without really being a part of it. One can even respect law and custom while standing above it. For instance, a man who has mastered humor would not respect the law from any sense of duty or tradition, but because he knows that disregarding the law, even for what appears to be justifiable reasons, usually creates social chaos - a totally useless phenomenon. There is, however, a serious disadvantage inherent in learning the secrets of humor's power. It would bind a man like Harry forever to the bourgeois. Any possibility of joining the Immortals would therefore be permanently lost. Harry stands at a crossroads. He may strive to master the power of humor and thus give up any hope of joining the Immortals, or he may continue his present life of discontent and suffering in hope of discovering the formula that will propel him into what the Treatise calls the starry cosmos.

We may point out that the cultivation of humor is in essence another of those shabby compromises, a halfway house where one may take refuge. The author of the Treatise appears to think that not only is Harry capable of attaining to the Immortals but also that he will be successful. For this reason, the Treatise continues Harry's analysis.

The Thousand And One Selves: The Treatise demolishes yet another of Harry's cherished myths. His stupid error has been to view himself as consisting of only one or two parts. This gross oversimplification has prohibited him from viewing himself in terms other than man-wolf. We recall that he attributes to his human nature everything that is noble, rational, and civilized, while he thinks his lupine nature encompasses the instincts, cruelty, and unrefined emotions. To further complicate his life, he regards these two selves as antithetical polarities constantly at war. He is convinced that the two parts are irreconcilable and that he is therefore destined to a life of suffering. Consequently, he feels a particular affinity to Goethe whose Faust exclaims: "Alas, two souls dwell in my breast."

The true cause of Harry's suffering is not that he has two souls but that he admits to having only two. He, as everyone else, is made up of thousands of selves. Yet mankind persists in perpetuating the fiction that the Self is a unit, one and indivisible. From time to time society is prepared to permit special individuals, such as Goethe, to have two selves and even worship him for it and write ponderous tomes about it.

The Treatise goes on to say that despite widespread opposition, the paraphernalia already exists for revealing the true nature of man's Self. The drama is most suitable although its possibilities have not been fully exploited. We may understand what is meant here if we regard the characters that a dramatist has created as different manifestations of his own Self. Taking Shakespeare as the example, we may say that Macbeth, Lady Macbeth, Macduff, even Hamlet and Iago are but single parts of the higher Self - Shakespeare's Self. Even the casual reader has an intuition of what the Treatise means, for it does not require a great deal of imagination to understand Macbeth's ambition, Iago's hatred, and Hamlet's indecision. Even if the reader cannot identify with the magnitude of their activities, he nevertheless acts out the same thing on a smaller scale every day.

So the lesson Harry must learn is that man is not made up of one or two selves, but of many thousands. In a way man resembles a puzzle made up of hundreds of parts, each playing its role and each claiming its due.

The Immortals: The last few pages of the Treatise contain some of the most important and difficult material in the novel. To complicate matters, there are elements of Nietzschean philosophy, Buddhist doctrine, and Jungian psychology. All are interwoven in such a way that Hesse has created from them an altogether new doctrine.

Harry is told that man in the ordinary sense of the word is not a fixed and static entity, the final result of millions of years of evolution, but a transition between nature and spirit. The only valid goal of man is to transcend his present condition and seek to rejoin the All, the realm of the Immortals. Here it is necessary to clarify what is meant by the All and the other expressions Hesse uses to refer to it, such as primal state of being, totality, the cosmos, the realm of pure spirit, the realm of the Immortals, and the starry cosmos. The All is a principle of metaphysics according to which man is said to have an innate, fixed position in the universe. In our present state of development the All is incomprehensible to us. But it is believed that a formula, such as a certain way of life, or of thinking, can be found that will enable us to comprehend it. When a person has succeeded in embracing the All he becomes a part of it. Then, with perfect clarity, he understands the meaning of his existence and his purpose in the whole scheme of things. Through this knowledge he will experience a pure and perfect happiness. In the All polarities are not merely reconciled; they do not exist. Even the concept of sin would be alien to this realm because sin implies its opposite, innocence. Although the Treatise carefully excludes Christianity, we may better understand what is meant by comparing the experience of totality to the state of innocence and pure harmony that man is said to have enjoyed before the Fall.

The Treatise goes on to point out that man can join the ranks of the Immortals through the process of individuation. That is, he must seek his innermost nature, affirm it, and live in harmony with it. When men realize the necessity of knowing themselves, progress toward totality is possible.

The Treatise explains further that the reason men find themselves in their present condition is because all living things when born are automatically guilty. Not guilty in the sense that some law has been transgressed, but that in a previous existence we failed in our quest of the All. In other words, every rebirth into the world, whether man, plant, or animal, is a sign that it is separated from the All and therefore in a way is guilty. This is one cause of man's despair and suffering. His life, his religions, and his philosophical systems are a record of his efforts to regain the All. So it is man's destiny to be reborn over and over again until he breaks out of the cycle of metempsychosis and takes the universe into himself. Unfortunately, man's soul is too small. It has lost its elasticity. It can, however, be distended through the process of painful individuation until it is large enough, or better, worthy enough, to contain it.

Thus the Christian idea is rejected that the solution lies in going backward to the innocence of childhood, to nature. Rather the road leads onward into life, further into sin and degradation. The Treatise states that above all, man must cease his attempts to "simplify" the Self and seek to "complicate" it. That is, man should not struggle to define the Self as consisting of one or two single parts but seek to discover more and more of his many thousands of selves. As the process of individuation reveals deeper and deeper insights into himself and into the scheme of things, the person frees himself from all shackles of life. He understands the relativity of all values and polarities. In short, he comprehends the incomprehensible. The Immortals have done this.

We now understand why Harry hesitates to begin the journey toward the Immortals. He knows that individuation requires the stripping away of the false conceptions that he has constructed around himself - most of which are hidden in the unconscious - until the true Self stands naked and alone. The true Self, he will then discover, is itself not a unity but is made up of many thousands of parts. Harry hesitates to commence this process because it is as spiritually painful as the stripping away of skin from a living body is physically disagreeable. He might be willing to clench his teeth and go through with it once, but he also knows that immortality is not to be had on such easy terms. The flaying of the Self is a ritual that must be performed innumerable times. Harry despairs because he realizes that in refusing to give himself up to individuation and bear the pain that his final death as a bourgeois requires, his life will be a living death. But on the other hand, he fears the agony that awaits his next step forward.

The Treatise addresses itself only to Harry's intellect. It points out the way; it is not the solution. The next step is the internalization of this intellectual cognition through experience. To even approach the unconscious, Harry must have in addition to intellect the three other tools of self-knowledge: intuition, sensation, and emotion. These will be provided by Pablo, Maria, and Hermine who will give him the help he needs for his voyage into the unconscious.

First Reaction: Harry's first reaction to the Treatise is one of hostility. He is quite familiar with the process of individuation but there seems to be no end to it. Long ago he chose to take the lonely way to the true self, but he discovered that the anguish far exceeded anything he had imagined. To be sure, each new shattering of the old self provided deeper insights and added to his wisdom, but each rebirth was accompanied by more loneliness and estrangement. A little more wisdom and a little more freedom seems hardly worth a lot more loneliness.

Harry reflects that the invisible rewards of his efforts have been bought at an enormous price and are perhaps not worth it. In his present, depressed state of mind, he even regrets that he has lost respect for the traditional values of God, country, and motherhood and that his youthful awe of science, professors, and the arts has turned into disillusionment. Above all he misses the security of the belief he once had that these men were constantly engaged in intrinsically worthwhile activities. To sum up, in the light of what self-discovery reveals, he sees little cause to continue. As might be expected, Harry's thoughts turn again to suicide. What Harry has failed to understand in the Treatise is that the happiness and the sense of fulfillment that accompanies attainment of totality comes only at the moment of breakthrough. Regrettably, there is no gradual diminishing of the suffering as one gets nearer the goal. The reverse is true. The closer one comes, the more unbearable the pain.

Yet Harry's mind is less occupied with the Treatise than with the vision announcing the Magic Theater. It is significant that he refers to the sign with the dancing letters as a "hallucination" rather than by a more objective term, because in so doing he indicates that he is aware that the true nature of what he saw was a premonition and not an actual sign.

One day he falls in with a funeral procession and from idle curiosity follows it to the cemetery. When the ceremony is over, Harry catches sight of someone whom he mistakes for the placard-bearer. Overtaking him, he asks if there is to be a show that night. The stolid citizen, who is not the placard-bearer after all, indignantly replies that he ought to go to the Black Eagle if he wants to satisfy his needs. As Harry later discovers, the Black Eagle is a notorious cafe and gathering place for call girls. But before he accidentally goes there, he has an experience that completely shatters him.

The Professor's House: This **episode** fulfills two functions in the novel. It gives us an opportunity to observe how Harry's dual nature operates under ordinary circumstances, and it makes him receptive to Hermine whom he meets that same evening.

Arriving in front of the house, Harry constructs an image of the professor's life and so puts himself into a vicious frame of mind. The professor represents everything that is wrong with teaching and scholarship. He believes in the acquisition of knowledge for its own sake and so thinks an education means committing to memory vast numbers of facts and so confuses education with the wisdom of experience. Likewise, scholarship consists in publishing annotated texts so as to contribute to the store of knowledge. His specialty is oriental mythology, but it never occurs to him that studying it as a manifestation of the unconscious or the collective unconscious could contribute to a fuller understanding of humanity which in turn could enable individuals to better understand themselves. He is an example of the pedantic scholar who has been educated beyond his intelligence. A comparison of Harry and the professor underscores the vastness separating the merely educated from the wise. The professor understands nothing of the causes of the war or the changes it brought about. Nor is he able to see that it is precisely his chauvinistic attitude that will be among the causes of the next war. Harry enters the house in a wrathful state.

The evening ends in disaster and is a total victory for the wolf. Once inside, a picture catches his eye which immediately irritates him. Following a dismal and strained dinner, Harry decides to make an end of the farce. He takes up Goethe's picture and attacks it, thereby wounding the hostess. He then tells the professor he had lied when he said that he had been in the city only a few days when in fact it had been several months. Furthermore, the professor had severely wounded him in agreeing with the article in the jingoist, reactionary newspaper.

And, in addition, newspapers of this type have no business in the hands of so-called learned men. Seizing his hat and coat, Harry storms out of the house leaving behind a bewildered and outraged host.

This **episode** is the occasion for an orgy of self-contempt, severe depression, and melancholy. It is particularly significant because it is his final defeat as a human being. He at last understands that there is no longer any hope of coming to terms with the bourgeois. As the magnitude of his alienation dawns for the first time, his thoughts turn once again to suicide. This time it appears that he will be unable to control the impulse, that once he returns to his rooms, he will be seized by a force stronger than his own and be compelled to cut his throat. He roams about the wet streets in terror, enters bars and drinks. As he runs aimlessly through the streets, he tells himself that even if cowardice prevented the deed today, the courage of self-contempt would succeed tomorrow. Why not get it over with as soon as possible. Harry's rescue comes from a totally unexpected quarter.

Hermine: Finding himself in a distant section of the city, he enters a cafe, the Black Eagle. There he meets Hermine who immediately takes charge of him. Hermine is a high-class call girl wise in the ways of her own world. Highly intelligent, she has mastered all the skills of her trade. She has made a careful study of men and knows from experience the most effective way of dealing with overwrought and agitated males like Harry. Moreover, she can usually tell at a glance just what is on a person's mind. When Harry sits down beside her, she concludes from his wet shoes, rumpled clothes, and the wild look in his face that he is in a very bad way and needs her. In fact, it appears as if she already knows everything about Harry. She guesses the reason he fears to go home, that he is overeducated, and that he needs to be mothered. She forces him to tell her about his experience at the professor's house and why he wants to kill himself. She responds to the story in just the right way. Instead of pretending sympathy or debating the problem intellectually, she makes fun of it and ends by calling him a big baby.

And so Hermine succeeds in dispelling Harry's thoughts of the previous hour. She mothers him, orders him about, and admonishes him. Her cleverness, wit, insight into human nature, and lively manner put Harry into a surprisingly cheerful frame of mind. In fact, even the reader soon finds himself wondering what a girl like her is doing in a place like this. Although it is not until later that Hermine tells Harry her background, it will be well to speak of it here.

From the little that is revealed, we know that she was born into the lower classes. It is difficult for the modern American student to appreciate the division of classes that prevailed in Europe until very recently and the role this played in determining a person's life. If, for example, a man was born into the proletariat, he was obliged to remain in that class the rest of his life regardless of whatever intelligence and special talents he possessed. We are not speaking of the highly gifted who find their way out, but of that vast number of individuals of above average intelligence who find the direction of their life determined at the moment of birth. Hermine is such a person. Gifted, sensitive, and beautiful, she would have been destined for great things had she been from the upper classes. Yet all that she could hope for was a life of drudgery as a shop clerk, exhausted from overwork, and cut off from all the beautiful luxuries that accompany money and position. Thus it is not surprising that after taking a good look at the dismal life of her neighbors and friends who are worn out from childbirth and old before their time, she decided to take the only way out that was open to her.

Even becoming a call girl of fairly good taste was hard enough. It is for this reason that she understands only too well Harry's disillusionment with life. Sensing this, Harry begs her to return to his table after she has danced.

Goethe: While Hermine is dancing, Harry falls asleep at the table and has a remarkable dream. He dreams that he is in an anteroom awaiting an interview with the poet Goethe. Harry's dream is, of course, symbolical, composed of pieces of his recent experiences. Goethe emanates from the events at the professor's house, while the reference to his "Immortal" status comes from the Treatise. Harry's use of the words "we young people" indicates his feeling of rejuvenation in the presence of Hermine. The transformation of the leg into the scorpion recalls not only the way Hermine's skirt brushes against his knees but it also signifies his ambivalent sexual feelings toward her. He desires her but at the same time he fears the consequences. Harry has always feared sexy young girls like Hermine because they represent feeling and passion, two things he rejects in favor of rationalism. Until now, he believed that only the cultivation of the spirit led to a meaningful existence.

In the dream, Goethe laughs at Harry for his inability to eschew his bourgeois prejudices and incapacity to look for deeper meaning beneath appearances, and so he commits the error of judging character by occupation. It would never occur to Harry that a prostitute might be capable of profound insight because that simply does not coincide with his preconceived notions about what ought to be on a prostitute's mind. And so another myth of his youth is demolished.

After this encounter with Hermine, Harry's attitude is completely transformed. Formulating the significance of what has happened to him, we conclude that the prospect of his future relationship with Hermine will not be an idle love affair. Here at last he has met someone who is able to penetrate the wall he has erected around himself, a human being who understands him, likes him, and stretches out a warm helping hand. For the first time in many years he has something to involve him, something to look forward to. Most important of all, he realizes that she is the way out of his isolation and soul sickness, the pinpoint of light at the end of the tunnel. What Harry needs is not more insight and more abstractions, but life, feeling and impulse, to live in the world and take part in it.

Hermine As Anima: Although they meet only for the second time, Hermine has an immediate and profound effect on Harry. It seems to him that he has known her all his life and so he does not hesitate to unburden himself to her. He immediately wants to know her name and when she asks him to guess, he says Hermine because she reminds him of Hermann, a friend of his youth. (The names here are significant: Hermine, Hermann, Harry Haller, Hermann Hesse.) Here it should be pointed out that Harry's relationship with Hermine will take place on two levels. While Hermine is a real person on the level of ordinary reality, Harry begins to project his feminine self, or anima upon her. We recall that in Jungian psychology, the anima acts as a filter between the conscious and the unconscious and dictates what information is conveyed from one to the other. By confronting the anima, we can look into the depths of the mind and know what is there. Jung goes on to say that the anima is an essential part of man and as such cannot be ignored. If a man tries to ignore it, or refuses to come to some sort of understanding with it, he will suffer from moods, inexplicable impulses and irritations. Therefore, since Hermine is the anima presented as an independent personality he can, by coming to terms with her, confront his own anima. Furthermore, he cannot put her off as easily as he does the Treatise.

Harry's Humanization: Harry has to learn how to play and Hermine can instruct him. She will teach him naive experience, how to enjoy the little things of everyday reality such as eating, drinking, and dancing. He must become a master at extracting the greatest delight from the most fleeting pleasure. But while Harry needs her to teach him the refinements of living, she needs him for something equally important. She promises to give him many orders that will be good for him and give him much pleasure. But in the end she will give him one final command which he will not find so delightful.

First, she will use all the resources of her profession to make him fall in love with her. When this has happened she will order him to kill her and he will obey. Hermine's words are open to two interpretations. She may mean that he will kill her in the ordinary sense of the word or she may refer to a symbolical act in which he will murder her image. This problem will be treated in more detail after we have examined the circumstances preceding the actual deed which occurs near the end of the Magic Theater. In any case, Hermine does not illuminate us as to the real meaning, for she breaks off the discussion to enjoy the dinner. Among the many things for which Harry admires his new friend, it is her capacity to pass from the most deadly serious subjects to the most lighthearted and frivolous ones without spoiling the pleasure of either. Harry's first lesson, Hermine says, is how to enjoy a meal. She explains that one does not merely squat and gobble so as to satisfy the appetite; but rather he should learn to concentrate all his attention on the pleasure of the moment in much the same way he applies himself to solving a difficult problem in aesthetics.

And Harry begins his dancing lessons in the firm conviction that it will be an exercise in futility. In order to be a proficient dancer, he thinks that one must have a firm and supple body along with a frivolous disposition. Much to his own surprise, he is not only able to learn the fox-trot during his first lesson but he even gets some pleasure out of the second one. Even so, this does not prevent him from being terrified the moment Hermine announces they will go dancing the next day. Harry's next lesson in bringing his life into better balance will take place, appropriately enough, at the Balances Hotel.

Harry's first hesitating steps into this new world are met by an onrush of disturbing and disintegrating influences which, now free of repression, threaten to overwhelm his carefully preserved intellectual realm. When new selves appear daily and demand to be recognized, they create chaos and confusion. Harry comes to realize what an illusion his former personality had been. He had developed and refined a few of his talents and then assigned to the Steppenwolf all that did not coincide with his view of an educated and sensitive humanist. Although this revelation is no frolicsome delight, Harry discovers that the destruction of his carefully nurtured misconceptions about himself and the reorganization of his personality provides unexpected new insights. Seeing himself in perspective, he is appalled at the hypocrisy of his former existence. How, for instance, was he able to so delude himself that he could condemn the power of industry while at the same time own stock in respectable corporations and live off the interest? And what of intellectual honesty if on the one hand he could protest against the war and preach brotherly love and on the other he is not willing to receive a few blows on his own head for his beliefs? It is precisely such self-disgust that compels Harry to continue seeking even though he knows every new experience and every new acquaintance will reveal yet another loathesome paradox that will require another painful reorganization.

Pablo: The saxophonist Pablo requires the greatest readjustment from Harry. When he first meets the musician, Harry cannot understand Hermine's admiration for him. He seems to be a jaded sensualist with bad taste in music, loud clothes, psychedelic drugs, and sex - a pretty but vacuous cretin whose primary concern in life consists in looking beautiful, pleasing women, and playing jazz, a form of music that reminds Harry of the steam from raw meat. Most irritating of all is the inane smile with which he greets Harry's musical theories. Yet Harry's appreciation and even fondness of Pablo increases as he learns the refinements of eating, dancing, and lovemaking. Pablo, it is revealed, is also a musician of the body. Highly skilled in the mixing and ministering of narcotics, he has a preparation suitable for dispelling every discomfort. He has specifics for stimulating the senses in various combinations and for heightening the intensity of the most trite experience. It is not long before Harry realizes that Pablo's shallowness is deceptive. Although he has not read any books, he possesses extraordinary intuitive wisdom. In contrast to Harry, Pablo lives in perfect harmony with his world of jazz and superficialities and is at absolute peace with himself. More importantly, he knows nothing of that split personality from which Harry suffers. As it later develops, Pablo is shown to be the ideal of the perfect man - an Immortal. Although Harry suspects Pablo's true nature quite from the beginning, he is not yet ready to scrutinize his own carefully constructed theories of art and beauty. The first serious doubt is occasioned by an argument about the relative values of music. Harry claims that modern music is an insipid and trivial wasteland while that of Mozart and Beethoven has depth and is eternal. Furthermore, what now passes for music is devoid of such refinements as counterpoint, tone, and thematic development. Pablo would know this if he took the time to learn something about musicology. Pablo replies that neither the musician nor the average listener requires an education in musicology for a particular melody, classical or modern, to get into the blood. Harry, of course, cannot permit himself to affirm the validity of this viewpoint because to do so would render much of his knowledge superfluous. In other terms, it would require another of those self-confrontations which he finds so disagreeable.

Harry acknowledges that the German spirit is dominated by the matriarchate (the belief in the mother-woman as the ultimate source of knowledge) and that these tendencies are revealed most vividly in the Germanic obsession for music. The modern intellectual has cultivated mood and feeling at the expense of his practical gifts. As a result, the intellectuals are not only ill at ease in reality; they are hostile to it; they have refused to put their talents into the service of mankind.

Maria: Maria, of course, is Hermine's gift. We remember that Hermine told Harry that he needed to discover what it is like to love as a human being rather than in his usual tragic and idealistic way. Maria is well equipped to be his instructor for she lives solely for love. She is to love and to the senses what Harry is to the intellect.

Through Maria, Harry gets a look into the circle of call girls, musicians, and refined hedonists. He discovers that most of them left poor homes to live on their easy virtue in order to enjoy the good life. Most of the girls, and Maria was one of them, existed solely for love, often with both sexes. Intelligent and yet thoughtless, the inhabitants of this strange twilit world lived out the short summer of their youth in gay abandon not caring, but knowing quite well, that a miserable end awaited them. The demimonde of night clubs, bars, and hotel lounges that Harry had always regarded as corrupt was to them the real world, neither good nor evil. Strangely, in their way they had learned the relativity of morality and values and had broken free of their attachment to the bourgeoisie.

In the following weeks Maria gives him many lessons in love, provides him with new insights, and new understanding, many of which prove to be painful. For instance, Maria's enthusiastic admiration for an American hit song all but demolishes Harry's carefully constructed aesthetics. Her childlike emotional response to Yearning, he sees, was just as genuine, pristine, and exalted an artistic experience, and perhaps even more intense, as the ecstasy felt by the learned Mozart connoisseur at a performance of Don Giovanni. Harry is profoundly shaken by this experience for he had always claimed that the greater the music the greater the enjoyment. He is further surprised to see that Maria's face glows with delight at the slightest pleasure, whether a bottle of wine or a new trinket. He reflects that such response is no less intense and genuine than a knowledgeable academe's rapture upon discovering one of Goethe's unpublished letters. At this point Harry begins to reflect upon the premise that education is a necessary preparation for a full life. Although Maria does not think and probably confines any reading she does to comic books, this does not diminish the intensity of her life. Why? Because Maria is a master at the art of living.

She teaches Harry that such items as perfume, rakish hats, and dainty purses are not tasteless baubles invented by an avaricious fashion industry for the purpose of exploiting the gullible but are the instruments by which one imparts life to a dull and drab world. Most importantly, Maria teaches Harry her great secret, the ability to experience life with the innocence of a child and to perceive the world through the senses. Harry proves to be an apt pupil. In her arms he discovers lovemaking without feelings of guilt and sin. Moreover, obliged to participate in Maria's activities in her youthful, lighthearted way, Harry is himself rejuvenated. The results of this brief relationship are so far-reaching that memories of the women he had known, long suppressed because they were painful, suddenly spring to mind and for the first time, he is able to accept them as integral parts of himself and in so doing, he is able to harmonize yet another discordant element of his Self.

By this time, the role of sex and women in the balancing of Harry's personality has been made clear. Sex is presented in a new light in that the process of individuation is initiated through lovemaking. Naturally, individuation does not consist in sensual refinement; it means advancement to a higher level of perception. Thus Harry is lifted up through sex and is enabled to affirm that half of his personality he had always denied.

The doctrine of redemption through sex, narcotics, and prostitutes may not strike the modern student as particularly noteworthy or even surprising. But if we consider the morality prevailing during the first decades of this century, we can better understand the radical nature of Hesse's ideas. It must have appeared strange indeed to readers brought up with Biblical stories of the Prodigal Son that a man could find salvation in anything other than spiritual illumination. In many traditional stories, the low point of the hero's development occurs when he goes into the world and squanders his fortune in licentious debauchery and is scarred for life by a single episode of riotous living and dissipated profligacy. All too frequently women were portrayed as blood-sucking vampires whose only pleasure lay in corrupting innocent young men. Furthermore, sex was widely regarded as a loathesome and sinful practice to be resisted more than indulged in. Not surprisingly, many people looked upon prostitutes and homosexuals as little more than human vermin.

The Immortals And Eternity: Harry's entrance into Hermine's world is to culminate at the annual masked-ball organized by a society of artists. The day before the ball Hermine visits Harry in his rooms where a remarkable conversation takes place. Harry tells Hermine that although he has been exceedingly happy in the last few weeks, he is nonetheless dissatisfied. He explains that he longs for unhappiness. He longs for the bittersweet, creative suffering that will make him willing and eager to die. In other words, he is ready and even impatient to commence the last phase of self confrontation that, no matter how painful, will end in the final death of the old Harry. His soul cannot be satisfied with the contentment and happiness of Maria's pleasure garden as long as he knows that with his new insights and new abilities he can try once again to join the ranks of the Immortals. This is something Hermine understands, for she too longs for death. Here it must be pointed out that the references to death signify the destruction or "death" of the old self through the process of individuation, not dying in the physical sense of the word. Hermine tells Harry that death is the only constructive alternative to existence in modern society.

Both of them in their youth had looked upon life enthusiastically, worshipped the beautiful and the sublime, and had idealistic faith in mankind. But their faith has found no outlet, their reverence no object, and their striving useless. Society, they discovered, does not ask for heroism and sacrifice. Whoever expects more from life than eating and drinking is a fool. Hermine, too, wanted more from life. She was talented and intelligent and had dreams, but all that was permitted to her was to be a fairly successful call girl. Nevertheless, people like Harry and her can find peace in this world in what she calls "eternity." It is the kingdom of truth where the music of Mozart and the deeds of the saints are found. It is not a place in time or in space, but a state of mind. We can be in eternity while living our present lives. Harry's and Hermine's true home is not in the world of refined triviality, but there with the Immortals. That is why they long for death.

Two Levels Of Perception: Reflecting on this conversation later that day, it seemed to Harry that it was not Hermine who had spoken to him, but that he was listening to his own thoughts. Here again we encounter the two levels of perception. Although Hermine, Maria, and Pablo are real persons, Harry's mind gives them an extra dimension which makes them symbols of his own ideas. This can be made clearer if we consider what Hesse had to say about the way people read.

There are three kinds of readers. The first accepts the book at face value, neither interpreting nor inferring. The second group reads like children with a child's imagination. The third, and most important for our purposes, is the person whose mind is stimulated by the book into seeing hundreds of personal connections, ideas, and inspirations. Such people no longer read what is on the page in front of them but translate the material in relationship to the myriad impressions, and experiences of their own lives. Hesse says that to such people even a magazine advertisement can be a revelation. It is in this way that Harry responds to his friends. The articulate conversation and penetrating insights evinced by Pablo and Hermine amount to no more than remarks onto which Harry transplants his own thoughts. We should also remember that Harry is recounting the story as he remembers it, not necessarily as it happened.

The Masked Ball: Harry's excited anticipation of the events in store for him the evening of the ball turn into fright when he arrives at the Globe Rooms. On one level, the dread is due to the fact that he is to figure there as an active participant rather than in his usual role as idle spectator. On the other hand, it is the fear of yet another self-confrontation. Once inside, the tumult, deafening clamor, and masses of people immediately put him out of humor. When he is about to leave, he receives a note that Hermine is in hell. The jamboree which a few moments previously had seemed to be an uncouth and rowdy fertility rite is now transformed into an intoxicating bacchanalia. Now the air no longer reeks of stale smoke and cheap wine but is the scent of perfume. Harry is so swept up by the music, the laughter, and the frenzy that he abandons himself to the general spirit. When he finally arrives in hell, the festive spirit has completely transformed the foul mood of the previous hour.

Hermine The Transvestite: As it turns out, hell is the hotel basement appropriately decorated in black with an orchestra of furiously playing devils. The terms which Harry uses to describe his sensations indicate that his descent into the underworld is symbolic of his descent into the hell of his unconscious where he will confront and come to terms with several repressed elements in his unconscious. He seats himself at the bar and mistakes a fellow sitting there for his childhood friend Hermann. On closer scrutiny, it is Hermine disguised as a young man. Under her hermaphroditic spell and without any particular effort on her part, Harry immediately falls in love with her. Thus, the first portion of Hermine's prophecy is fulfilled.

Hesse employs hermaphroditism in *Steppenwolf* as a symbol of totality, the reconciliation of opposites. Although he again betrays Jung's influence, the concept extends back to the symbols of coupled male and female gods in primitive mythology. It is therefore appropriate that as Harry's anima, Hermine should combine both the male and female elements of his Self. The hermaphroditic **theme** recurs at significant points in the novel. When Hermine's boyish face reminds him of someone from his youth, we recall that she and Maria freely admit to a lesbian relationship, and that Pablo once suggests a love orgy for three. Harry does not participate, but he at least understands homosexual love and is able to see that even there polarities must cease. It is worth noting that he nevertheless fantasizes the love orgy through suggestion under the spell of one of Pablo's narcotic cocktails. Later he remembers, somewhat uncomfortably, the thousand selves of the Treatise. At the ball, the transvestite Hermine teaches the bourgeois Harry to recognize the hermaphroditic nature of his own soul and in so doing, that of all men. This is an essential lesson, for he had always looked upon homoeroticism as the ultimate stage of human degradation. Now Harry and Hermine are able to speak freely of those years in early youth when the erotic capacity embraces both sexes and imbues the sensual and spiritual with love.

As the ball increases in intensity, Harry again learns something familiar to almost everyone, the dissolving of the individual personality into the crowd. The music, the dancing, and the teeming throng become an intoxicating delirium. For hours he swirls through the giddy, unreal world feeling the mystic union with the mass and the release of the Self.

In the early hours of the morning Hermine reappears dressed as a woman. She and Harry perform a symbolic wedding-dance that is a prelude to their "marriage." At the beginning of their relationship, Hermine had decreed that sex between them must be put off until they were in love. As Harry's anima, sex will be more than physical. It will be emotional and spiritual, the union of the animus and the anima as well as signifying Harry's success in harmonizing his personality. Clasping his bride, Harry feels how all the women of that evening, those whom he had desired and those with whom he had danced, were all dissolved into Hermine. Later they accompany Pablo to a room on the top floor of the building. The descent into the underworld is now contrasted to the ascent into what Harry calls an atmosphere of very thinned-out reality. Pablo passes round some long, thin cigarettes (probably opium mixed with marijuana). The last stage of Harry's education is about to begin.

The new experiences and insights of the past few weeks, the Treatise and the masked ball all prepared Harry for the final step: the confrontation with the unconscious and the repressions, fears, and instinctive impulses lodged there. Pablo becomes the dominant force who will lead Harry into the deepest labyrinth of his Self. During this time, he is no longer the saxophonist but functions as the omniscient and omnipotent Magus archetype.

On the level of everyday reality the Magic Theater is an opium fantasy experienced in a deserted theater. But, in Harry's mind, it becomes a fantastic odyssey through the unconscious. The line separating illusion and reality is effaced and, since time is also suspended, Harry finally understands the simultaneity of such phenomena as past and present, wish and fulfillment.

Illusion And Reality: Since the object of the Magic Theater is to show Harry the way to the Immortals, one of the many things he must learn is not to view the world in polarities. To accomplish this, he must understand with the wisdom of experience that opposites exist only in the human mind. First illusion and reality, the greatest of all polarities, are presented in such a way that they are no longer separable. So adroitly has Hesse managed his task that even the reader experiences these phenomena as one. He finds himself unable to distinguish between what actually happens and what merely appears to happen. This technique enables the author to use the reader's own mind to show him the fallacy of polarization. In fact, if the letters Hesse received from his readers are any indication, the vast majority of his audience regarded the marvelous events of the Magic Theater as actual occurrence.

The Magic Theater: Each sideshow develops and reconciles a motif appearing earlier in the novel. Looking into the magic mirror, two of his selves spring out. One leaps laughingly into Pablo's arms and goes off with him, and the other hurls himself into the booth called All Girls Are Yours. (We recall that Pablo is proficient in lovemaking with both sexes.) Harry now sees that one facet of his personality is eager to explore homoeroticism while the other is anxious for the heterosexual experience. Since he later returns to the same booth and enjoys the love of every girl he ever knew, the resolution of polarity in physical love is indicated.

The Great Automobile Hunt: Inside, he discovers that the world is again at war, but with a new twist. The battle rages between the adherents of technological progress and those who want to abolish the unfeeling machines, especially the automobile. Harry then meets Gustav, a friend of his youth, and they go off to the mountains where they stop and climb a tall tree growing by the highway. Here Harry the confirmed pacifist discovers yet another part of his personality. With intense excitement the two friends take pot shots at passing cars and joyfully watch as they break through the guard rail and plunge into the abyss. Much to his own surprise, he enjoys the sport immensely. Harry finds this war particularly gratifying since it provides a chance to give physical expression to his hatred of technology.

Hesse believed that technological progress, represented by the obsession with the automobile and other mechanical contraptions, is responsible for the lack of soul in the modern world. Machines and gadgets in themselves do not corrupt the human spirit, but the worship of them does. It leads to trivialization of the soul, to the engendering of false values, and to the impoverishment of life. Furthermore, our machinery and factories mean a nightmarish loss of identity and the transformation of the spirit into rapacious hedonism. The auto hunt is Hesse's dream of liberating man from the unfeeling, sinister technology that will permanently deprive man of happiness.

Late in life a friend asked Hesse what he thought about the future of mankind. He replied that "...in fifty years the earth will be a graveyard of machines, and the soul of the astronaut will simply be the cabin of his own rocket." We may better understand Hesse's aversion to technology if we view the problem in different terms.

Suppose one's spiritual goal in life is to attain a sense of fulfillment and happiness. Then suppose he decides that owning his own home and car are essential to this end. Whether he wishes it or not, he has made the house and car the emblems of his spiritual goal and, in so doing, has lost sight of the original goal and is only pursuing the emblem. By confusing the material object with the spiritual one, he relinquishes personal control over his happiness because if he cannot keep up the payments for some reason his house will be repossessed and his happiness along with it. Thus Hesse is saying that in the modern technological society, man has lost sight of true values and pursues objects instead.

The auto hunt teaches the arch-rationalist Harry that any kind of meaningful, responsible life cannot be based solely on reason and duty, but has to be tempered with intuition and feeling. He listens to a conversation between Gustav and the Attorney General whom they have just shot. He replies to

Gustav's accusations that he was not personally responsible for the death sentences and oppressive treatment of society but that it was simply a matter of acting in accordance with duty. This is a dangerous distortion of the concept. The tendency to hide behind duty, rules, and laws is typical of the modern fear of making a free choice between alternatives and accepting the responsibility. When decision-making is deprived of feeling and emotion, life becomes brutalized and the human mind is reduced to the same functional level as a mechanical apparatus. Duty should be abolished, for then men would know personal guilt for their actions and so be more careful of their decisions.

Both Harry and Gustav believe that in principle they are doing the right thing even though it is childish and irrational, just as war is childish and irrational. Harry understands for the first time that a war is not fought for rational reasons, but because it is fun. Furthermore, he sees that reason as a basis for civilization is untenable. This is so because the fault of reason is that it seeks to simplify everything. It is not content until it has reduced to the lowest common denominator every fact, every experience, and everything believed on the evidence of religion, feeling, tradition, and authority. Applied to man, reason strives to separate him into the simplest component parts in order to understand him. Once this has been accomplished, human behavior can be reduced to a set of tables, like the logarithms, predictive of every motivation, desire, and act. We recall that the Treatise rejects reason as the panacea to our ills because a meaningful life can be attained only by "complicating" the Self, not by "simplifying" it. The seeker must come to terms with the fact that reason alone is insufficient and that feeling, intuition, and the senses must be accorded their rights.

Constructing The Personality: Behind this door he learns the fundamental error of modern psychology. It is false to claim that the personality is a unit while in fact it is composed of a multitude of parts much as the human body is made up of innumerable cells. Yet society calls it madness to break the unity into its separate parts. Science is right in pointing out that multiplicity cannot be dealt with unless there is a specific series, but it is wrong to insist that there is only one possible order in which the parts may be arranged. Such oversimplification not only destroys the impulse to original thinking, but also allows many seriously deranged people to walk freely about the streets. As one way out of the dilemma, we must learn the art of soul-building. In other words, anyone who finds that he has been defeated by life and has thus "gone to pieces" can be taught to rearrange the pieces of his personality into a series better suited to playing the game. The possibilities are endless. We may take the parts of our disintegrated personality and construct innumerable new situations.

Harry is now given a visual demonstration of the Treatise's discourse on the thousand-and-one selves and is thereby enabled to internalize the knowledge as wisdom. The object of this lesson is to teach Harry the game of life. He learns that it is simply the ability to rearrange the parts of the Self to meet every new situation. The most successful lives will be led by those who have mastered the game. When one has become a proficient player, then any part of the Self which today suddenly grows out of proportion and threatens destruction, can be reduced to insignificance tomorrow by restructuring the rebellious elements.

Taming Of The Steppenwolf: Harry's most harrowing experience, however, occurs in the booth where he witnesses a dramatization of his old lupine personality. On the stage a trainer, who bears an unmistakable resemblance to Harry, puts a large wolf through a series of humiliating tricks. Then the wolf assumes the dominant role and degrades the trainer. Symbolic of Harry's identification with the two performers is the taste of chocolate and blood in his mouth when he dashes from the room in terror. For the first time, he sees how his systematic repression of normal thoughts, emotions, and primal urges has turned them into warped monstrosities.

All Girls Are Yours: Racing up and down the corridor in hopes of finding an experience that will dispel the effects of the Steppenwolf spectacle, he dashes into the room whose sign proclaims All Girls Are Yours. Harry, the frustrated lover, now makes up for all his missed chances. Beginning with his first love, Rosa Kreisler, Harry reexperiences each female relationship of his life, not as they were but as they should have been. Instead of dialectic and renunciation, new meaning is given. He learns how to heighten the intensity and value of experience by losing himself in it. Total immersion in experience does not imply that a person should throw up his life and devote himself to only one thing. Rather, he should learn the art of concentrating his attention entirely on the current activity to the exclusion of all else; i.e., when thinking, he should do nothing but think; when composing, he should do nothing but compose; and when loving, he should do nothing but love.

In this **episode**, Harry loves for the first time unperturbed by himself as a thinker who analyzes each sensation; he is not tortured by the Steppenwolf who perverts and destroys, and he is left in peace by the moralist who makes him feel guilty. Now that Harry has affirmed that the Self is composed of a multiplicity of parts, he next learns to respond to women in a multiplicity of ways, each according to one of the parts of his Self. He understands that any genuine relationship is based on taking from each woman what she has to give and in letting each woman take from him what she needs. Thus, instead of projecting an artificial image of himself, he learns to remain passive and let the other person call forth that particular part of his personality that most nearly coincides with that individual's needs. The reason for Harry's singular lack of success with women was that he had reacted in one of two predictable ways, as the Steppenwolf or as the ascetic intellectual.

Finally, Harry leaves this booth for the same reasons he left Maria. The object of his life is not to dwell forever in warm pleasure gardens but to seek the realm of the Immortals.

HOW ONE KILLS THROUGH LOVE

Guilt And Redemption: Once more in the corridor, he is startled by the sign that reads How One Kills Through Love. As he hears an icy, metallic laughter in the air, he is overcome with longing because its unearthly and eerie nature has been the symbol of the Immortals throughout the novel. At that moment, Pablo disguised as Mozart enters from one of the doors and proceeds to give Harry a brutal lesson in the nature of guilt.

He lightly explains that every individual incurs the guilt of his age in the same way a Christian incurs Original Sin. One is born and at once he is guilty. It is as simple as that. The fault of the last century and this one is that of superfluity.

The implications of such a view are frightening for it signifies forces at work over which we have no control and, in most cases, are not even aware of. Due to this new dimension, how is one to determine the extent to which the fault of his age is reflected in what he creates? How can one recognize it and then strive to be free of it? The Immortals know, of course, but their knowledge came only at the end of self-confrontation. When Mozart sees that his discourse has rendered Harry thoroughly miserable, he breaks out into the piercing frozen laughter of the Immortals and ridicules Harry for worrying about it. Harry still has not learned to laugh.

Hermine's Murder: If we compare the old Harry with the new, we see that he has made considerable progress toward breaking free of his bourgeois past. Yet, as the subsequent events prove, he still has a long way to go. When Harry reawakens from a faint, he goes looking for Hermine, feeling that he is at last ready to consummate the most important love of his life. Instead, he finds her and Pablo lying on the rug naked and asleep, obviously having made love. Harry notices a bite beneath her left breast into which he plunges his knife without a moment's hesitation. He wonders vaguely why she looks surprised.

At this point, the two levels of reality that have been growing nearer throughout the novel merge into one. It is no longer unequivocally clear what actually happens. Does Harry kill Hermine in the ordinary sense of the word, or is the deed a surreal act in which he destroys the image of her? The motivation behind the deed is equally debatable. There is perhaps no more hotly debated item in Hesse's writings. The problem is further complicated in that Hesse did not do us the favor of clarifying the issue. Until a yet unknown letter is discovered that throws more light on this **episode**, there will be as many interpretations as there are readers. It is here that the student encounters what the study of literature is all about. To come to a cogent and relevant conclusion, he must arrive at his own decision based not only on a careful examination of the textual evidence but he must also consider the event in relationship to Hesse's overall way of thinking. Since each of the existing interpretations have their valid points, we will present the chief viewpoints and hope that the student will use them as a basis for making his own decision.

One commonly held view claims that Harry does in fact kill Hermine. We remember that she tells Harry during their first dinner engagement that she is interested in him mainly because she wants him to kill her, and she knows that he will obey her eventual command to do so. It is therefore argued that Harry commits the act in obedience to her unspoken command. Furthermore, Hesse gives a lurid description of the blood flowing out over the carpet, describes how Pablo turns over a corner of the rug to hide the wound, and later comes precariously close to sitting in the pool of blood that has collected on the floor. And again, in a moment of lucidity near the end, Pablo says Harry's behavior has been a disappointment because he had abused the theater by "stabbing with knives and soiling our beautiful make-believe world with the mud of reality." Finally, it is noteworthy that Hesse was fond of ending his novels with the death of one of the chief protagonists. Demian dies in the war, Kamala succumbs to a poisonous snake, Hans Giebenrath and Klein both drown, Goldmund is thrown from a horse and dies of internal injuries, and Josef Knecht dies from heart failure after diving into an icy mountain lake. In short, the adherents of this interpretation insist that Hermine's death should be taken at face value.

The opposite view holds that Harry murders his beloved in a purely symbolical way. The deed belongs in the same realm of the fantastic as does the flickering sign above the gothic portal announcing the Magic Theater. We recall that Hesse uses a technical device of German Romanticism to make the fantastic appear as reality. The surreal is always constructed of material gathered from everyday events. Harry's eidetic transformation of it is then described in realistic terms. Through the constant juxtaposition of the real and the imaginary, the author may make the real appear fantastic or he may make the fantastic appear uncomfortably real. Therefore, it is obvious that even though Hermine does tell Harry that he will kill her, she means only that he will destroy their relationship because of his latent bourgeois intolerance toward prostitutes. Harry's double perception causes him to take her words literally. The "murder," then, amounts to no more than an expression of outrage, a momentary regression into his old bourgeois self. Further evidence in support of this view is that a knife is hardly an object one would carry to a masked ball. It will be recalled that the weapon had been mysteriously conjured from the pieces of Harry's personality that were in his pocket. Moreover, in the trial Harry is accused of stabbing to death "the reflection of a girl with the reflection of a knife." If more proof were needed, we can point out that Pablo suggests that they bring Hermine back to life - that is by apologizing - and marry her to Harry. In other words, what actually occurs in this **episode** is a symbolical murder of Hermine's image described in very real terms.

The reasons for Harry's action, however, are somewhat clearer. The explanation lies in what Hermine symbolizes for Harry. Both she and the Treatise tell him that he cannot hope to break out of this life into the starry cosmos until he has shed both his Steppenwolfian nature and his bourgeois veneer. He must learn that his personality, as every man's is not composed of one or two parts but of innumerable ones. The Immortals can be reached only by bringing the many discordant elements into harmony. He must peer into the depths of his soul and learn to affirm what he finds there. To point out that Harry had been unable to do this alone would be to belabor the obvious, because he has been struggling with this problem for most of his forty-eight years. Harry has arbitrarily polarized his world along the precepts of bourgeois morality, accepting those impulses that coincided with his image of a refined and educated humanist while all the rest were suppressed.

When Hermine first meets him at the Black Eagle, she intuitively knows the source of his malaise and, taking a genuine interest in him, decides to help. Along with Maria and Pablo, she shows Harry that all those parts of his Self which he had systematically repressed were the chief cause of his failure and suffering. She teaches him that morality and polarities are rational creations and do not exist apart from the mind that gave them birth. By the example of her own life, she proves that it is possible to affirm every aspect of the world and live in harmony with it. She is totally free of ethical absolutism. Clearly, then, Hermine is more than a teacher. She is the symbol of harmony that stands in contrast to Harry's polarized personality. Therefore, if Harry takes possession of Hermine it will be a sign that he has succeeded in balancing his personality. This is why she decreed that sex between them must be postponed until he is in love with her because that will be the symbol of harmony. It is significant that Harry is unable to love her until the moment he affirms the last polarity, hermaphroditism.

But the final consummation is not permitted to take place. The scene he witnesses between Pablo and Hermine is his greatest test. Of course, it requires little effort on our part to understand Harry's deeply wounded feelings when he finds the woman he loves in the arms of his friend. Yet his lesson in this case is that possessive love is just another factor of middle-class conditioning. Like Hermine and Maria, he must understand that it is possible to love many people at the same time without the feeling for one affecting that of the other. In the Magic Theater, he learns that not only can he love many women simultaneously, but also in many different ways, each according to one of his many selves. Even Maria tells him that she is able to have many lovers because she loves in many different ways. But although he understands this rationally, he is not able to transfer the knowledge to his personal feelings. Thus feeling and reason, the chief opposites of his life, remain polarized. Harry has failed, and the final symbolical union of their marriage cannot take place. Surprisingly, Pablo understands this as the subsequent events show.

Harry's Reaction: When Pablo wakes up and sees what Harry has done, his reaction is to smile, turn over a corner of the rug to hide the wound, and silently leave the box. Harry remains alone staring at Hermine. In some of the most beautiful lyrical prose he has written, Hesse describes Harry's sensations. Gradually, the body begins to exhale a wintry coldness which fills the room with an atmosphere of desolation and hopelessness causing Harry's limbs to grow numb. He realizes that in killing Hermine, he had extinguished the sun itself. Yet not once during the few minutes he is alone with her does he feel regret. In fact, he cannot come to any conclusion about the rightness or the wrongness of the deed. After a brief effort, he simply gives up thinking about it. He feels sad, depressed, and is vaguely afraid that Mozart and the chessplayer will be displeased. He is less interested in such thoughts than in marveling at the severe cold which grows in intensity until it reminds him of the Immortals and the music of Mozart. A frigid and rarefied atmosphere, cold metallic laughter blended with the wondrous, icy silence of absolute loneliness are all symbols of totality. In associating Hermine's death with his ultimate goal, he indicates that he regards the murder in a positive way.

The poem that suddenly occurs to him underscores this point. Unfortunately, the English translation has done more justice to the poetic qualities than to the meaning. Obviously the work of an Immortal, the verse defines totality as a state of superior indifference which, when attained, renders incomprehensible the concepts of time, youth, age, and even the apparently irreconcilable natural opposites, male and female.

The Immortals, it goes on to say, are able to sustain themselves in their kingdom through "cool, starbright laughter." It is revealing that cold, ice, and other related terms occur six times in the six lines of the poem. As a realm of objective indifference, it is appropriate that immortality should be described in terms of coldness for this most nearly corresponds to the sensation we associate with indifference. In the light of the foregoing, we can now better understand Harry's peculiar reaction to Hermine's murder. The fact that he does not reflect on the rightness of his act, that he feels no regret, and most significantly, that he places more emphasis on the increasing coldness than his feelings toward Hermine indicate his indifference to her as a person.

The Ideal Versus The Real: Harry's pleasant daydreams are interrupted by Mozart who returns with a primitive radio. After twisting and twiddling, he locates a broadcast of Handel's Concerto Grosso in F Major. Because of the interference and static, the music is terribly distorted and scarcely audible. Appalled and outraged, Harry exclaims that it is an abomination to subject such divine music to the mercy of modern technology. Harry must learn another lesson.

On the surface it appears that the radio is the ultimate weapon in the war between art and technology. Yet if one listens carefully, the original majesty of the music can be heard behind the distortion. Thus Harry is witnessing a dramatization of the eternal conflict between the ideal and the real.

Throughout history man has regarded his store of ideas as his most beautiful possession and he has continually sought ways to make them real, to bring them to life without destroying them in the process. Yet it has been man's fate that when the idea is taken from the abstract and given form in reality, the result is a saddening distortion of its original beauty. Most irritating, however, is that the radio cannot render the original depth and pristine purity, and, therefore, it robs music of dignity. Harry insists that if the reproduction is not perfect, the attempt should be abandoned. We may better understand Harry's feelings if we compare them to our own when television uses Beethoven's Fifth Symphony to advertise a popular brand of toilet-bowl cleaner. While it is somewhat difficult to visualize Harry Haller watching television, it is rather easy to imagine his reaction. This brings us to the point of Mozart's lesson. The croaking instrument cannot completely destroy the spirit and magnificence of the music. If Harry listens without mockery and pathos, he can hear the noble outline of Handel's concerto. So it is with life. What we call life is nothing but a picture of man's puny efforts to give form to the ideal. And if we are to preserve our sanity, we must learn to perceive life's original beauty behind its trivial image. In other words, we must learn what to take seriously and what to laugh at. Once again, Harry is taught the importance of laughter. It is the only weapon capable of reconciling life's discordant elements and which will allow a man to live and to create against all odds.

Harry's Trial And Execution: Despite the efforts of his teachers, Harry has not learned to laugh. This error has made his life miserable, warped his gifts, and poisoned the end of his most beautiful relationship. At first he makes a weak effort to wriggle out of the responsibility by blaming it all on Hermine. Was it not, after all, her own wish? But that fatuous explanation is demolished by Mozart's eerie, noiseless laughter. How, for instance, could he take Hermine's insights on time and eternity as extensions of his own thoughts, which in fact they were, while, on the other hand, he regarded her prediction of death as entirely her own, which it was not? Had he not guessed at her prediction even before she spoke? He is thoroughly miserable and dejected, because he does not know why he killed her.

But as Pablo indicates, ignorance of the motivation does not release one from the responsibility. Nor does Harry want to escape the consequences. He is only too eager to subject himself to the most horrible punishments to expiate his act. As long, that is, as the punishment is in accordance with the requirements of good tragedy. He longs to suffer nobly and eternally like Prometheus chained to the rock, or perhaps as blind Oedipus who wanders aimlessly through the barren wilderness for the remainder of his days. Or, as in a French romance, he will walk across an empty, echoing prison yard shrouded in the early morning mist and bare his neck to the headsman's axe. Ironically, Harry's trial and execution take place in just such surroundings.

The trial shows Harry the futility of despair. He is "condemned" to go on living because confrontation with reality is more important than resolution. He will see that his failure is due to insufficient self-knowledge, and he will accuse himself afresh. It is only by self-judgment that he can arrive at the recognition that it is his bourgeois self that has separated him from his inner self by splitting his individuality. Pablo has already explained that the Steppenwolf is still alive and that it must be totally destroyed if the true self is to be revealed. The important factor here is that Harry must understand the necessity of traversing the hell of the unconscious without losing sight of the goal. And do it without despair. All the events of the theater are events of his own psyche.

Harry's submission to his punishment signifies his readiness at this point to look behind the surreal images and accept the realities they contain. Harry is not accorded the luxury of physical punishment because that would release him from self-punishment. Instead, he is laughed at and refused entrance into the theater. That is, he is forbidden descent into the unconscious, a descent which he previously dreaded but now desires.

Laughter: If Harry is not to be destroyed by the world, he must learn to live in it and listen to its trivial music, cease taking life seriously, and give up viewing his position in it as a tragedy. Or better, internalize the Treatise's lesson that existence can be rendered bearable and productive only if one perceives the humor in it. It is the power of humor that enables a man to both live in the world without being a part of it and to conform to its requirements while rising above them. Finally, the individual must come to terms with the disagreeable fact that life requires absolutely nothing of its members and that it is cruelly indifferent to heroism, self-sacrifice, and creative activity. Regrettably, anyone who expects more from life than eating and drinking is a fool. The only alternative is to regard life in the same way Mozart has taught Harry to listen to the radio: Apprehend and honor the ideal and laugh at its corruption and distortion.

The novel ends on an optimistic note. Mozart becomes Pablo once again and they enjoy a final cigarette together. Even though he has not succeeded in learning the game of life this time, he will do better the next time.

As the thick smoke fills the room and Harry begins to hallucinate, it appears to him that when Pablo picks up Hermine she shrinks in his hands to the size of a cigarette. Perhaps, symbolically, Harry has transcended his last teacher and her significance in his present and future life as she shrinks and disappears into the same pocket from which his friend conjured the cigarette. Harry reflects that he has been brought to the point where he is not only willing but eager to traverse the hell of his inner being as often as necessary.

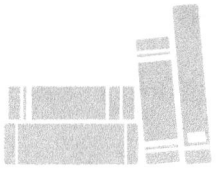

STEPPENWOLF

CHARACTERIZATION IN STEPPENWOLF

THE BOURGEOIS NARRATOR

The author of the Preface remains undeveloped because he is a type, not a character. He is a man of the middle class who lives in harmony with himself and with his environment. Proud of his healthy bourgeois attitude to life, he respects the police, he insists on personal cleanliness and a well-ordered, respectable existence. His world is founded on regularity in all things and is filled with practical duties and thoughts. He enjoys the contentment of middle-class security that comes from long years of self-discipline and respect for tradition. He readily admits to believing in moderation, hard work, and in an ordered life. He condemns atheists and extremists of all kinds and takes seriously posters depicting the bolshevik with the dagger between his teeth. He spends his leisure hours pursuing constructive projects such as assembling a radio from a mail-order kit. We see that he judges a person's character by the quality of his material possessions or the way in which he orders his life. For example, he disapproves of Harry's careless dress, and he is highly disturbed because the new lodger often stays in bed until noon. Furthermore, Harry has no practical employment. Anyone who does not earn his bread by the sweat of his brow is somehow suspect. The narrator's suspicions often lead him to snoop about Harry's rooms, and he dislikes both Harry's reading matter and the empty wine bottles and overflowing ash trays scattered about. As might be expected, he condemns alcohol because intoxication means a loss of control over one's thoughts and actions. Loss of control and living in extremes, even for very short periods, must be avoided at all costs.

In the Treatise Hesse defines the bourgeois. Such men refuse total commitment because it involves a loss of identity and it is precisely the Self which the bourgeois values above all else. Therefore, by carefully regulating his life, he establishes and maintains an equilibrium between the innumerable extremes of which human nature is capable. Although they may sympathize with Steppenwolfian creatures like Harry, they can never permit themselves to understand them because that would threaten their own system of values. They are by nature suspicious of change, individuality, and greatness. In times of social upheaval, these are the men who will follow the charismatic leader with tears in their eyes and will gladly lay down their lives for him. But they will end by hanging him and then erect monuments to exalt and worship him. Men like the narrator are conservative and law-abiding. They willingly live under control. Perhaps it is even their duty to be controlled because it is their vocation. The Steppenwolves inspire the world and lead it to new goals; the bourgeois merely preserves the world as it is and Populates it.

HARRY HALLER

Harry Haller is a forty-eight year old man who suffers all the aches and pains of middle age. He suffers from rheumatism in his joints, indigestion, and insomnia. He has lost faith in himself and humanity; he has nothing in common with the entire modern age whose values revolve around science, technology, and rapacious consumption. He has devoted his life exclusively to the cultivation of the spirit, the arts, humanities and everything that gives meaning to life but finds, instead of fulfillment, that his values and ideology have alienated him from society and have cut him off from any possibility of communion with his fellow men. He is reviled as a traitor and a coward by his countrymen for his pacifistic views and is dismissed as a crank for condemning the dehumanizing effects of technology. Having demanded and all but attained absolute freedom, he finds he is suffocating in the vacuum of his loneliness. He can go on living only by promising himself the luxury of suicide on the morning of his fiftieth birthday.

Shortly after we meet him, he comes into possession of "The Treatise on the Steppenwolf" which suggests that the true cause of his despair and anguish lies within himself, not within society. He is told that he is not free of the bourgeois morality which he so roundly condemns but is only alienated from it. If he is to live peacefully and productively in the everyday world, he must learn to view it with humor and peer into his soul and discover his inner Self. Not only would humor free him from his ambivalent love-hate relationship with the bourgeois, but it would make his life bearable and profitable. Unfortunately, learning the secrets of humor's power would bind him forever to the bourgeois. For that reason the Treatise suggests a second, more difficult, but vastly more rewarding alternative. He may choose instead to try for the realm of the Immortals by undergoing the process of individuation. He must seek to know the many thousands of selves that make up his innermost nature, affirm them and live in harmony with them. Although he makes no immediate choice, he eventually opts for the second alternative.

Soon after he reads the Treatise, Harry comes into contact with the world of Hermine and so begins the internalization of the Treatise's abstract knowledge. During the following month he learns the refinements of sensuality and affirms the validity of that world which he had always feared and rejected. Harry receives his final lessons in the marvelous events of the Magic Theater. His defenses effaced by Pablo's drugs, he undergoes a series of erotic and violent experiences which he would have indignantly rejected in his normal state of mind. Nevertheless, he is taught the essential lesson that he is not only capable of committing but (most importantly for his education) of enjoying every human act from the most savage and vile to the most noble and sublime. While he is able to dwell among the Immortals as long as he is sustained by narcotics, he reverts to his old bourgeois self when the effects wear off and, towards morning, murders Hermine when he finds her and his friend naked on the rug. As punishment for misusing the Magic Theater, he is hailed before a jury of Immortals who condemn him to live in the world until he learns what to take seriously in life and can laugh at all the rest, until he can play the game of life. Although the remnants of his bourgeois nature cause the failure, his education has been a success because he understands at the end that he can join the ranks of the Immortals as soon as he has brought the discordant elements of his Personality into harmony.

HERMINE

The highly intelligent, sensitive, and gifted Hermine has chosen the brief, easy life of the call girl in preference to the numbing drudgery for which her proletarian background destined her. At first, she was embittered that life and society had no use for her talents and that existence itself was unchallenging, meaningless, and trivial. Soon she realized that any kind of well-adjusted existence demands acceptance of the world as it is. Since life itself is trivial and meaningless, she reasons, one's existence in it should reflect this. Consequently, she has used her cleverness and insight to master the game of life and so extract from it the greatest pleasure. In other words, Hermine has defeated the world by accepting it on its own terms. She has seen the futility of imposing order where none belongs and understands with the wisdom of experience that polarization can only lead to dissatisfaction. Unlike Harry, she is free of the narrow bourgeois morality with its delicate balance between what is permitted and not permitted. Hermine's reconciliation of polarities accounts both for her profession and hermaphroditism.

It is no accident that Hesse chose prostitution and hermaphroditism as his examples because to traditional Western morality these appear as the most irreconcilable opposites of all. We must not miss Hesse's point. This is neither a paean to call girls and lesbians nor a veiled declaration of the author's own condition. Rather the object is to show the reader that even here polarities must cease.

Yet despite her vivacity and skillful ability to enjoy life, Hermine suffers the unhappiness of disillusionment. She says at one point that she will teach Harry how to be gay and enjoy life and remain unhappy, while he will teach her to think great thoughts and still be unhappy. She, like Harry, has an extra intellectual dimension that alienates her from the world. She, too, in her youth had looked upon life idealistically and had revered the beautiful and the sublime, but her faith and striving were useless for they had no outlet. She has finally realized that anyone who expects more from life than eating and sleeping or who prefers such things as music to noise and seeks genuine feeling to fleeting passion is out of place in this world. Not only has Hermine taken a genuine interest in Harry because she feels spiritually akin to him but because she sees that he too is struggling to escape from this existence into a better world. She sees that whereas he has the capacity to succeed, in order to do so he must learn to experience and to affirm everything life has to offer. Thus, she decides to help bring his life into balance by teaching him the refinements of living and by showing him that the life of the spirit is only part of the answer.

Hermine also functions as Harry's anima. After their first meeting, Harry looks upon her as the only person who can penetrate his shell and lead him out of his suicidal existence. As the novel progresses, Harry increasingly projects his anima onto her so that by the end of the masked ball when they perform their nuptial dance, Harry imagines that all his partners of the evening had melted into Hermine. Her transformation into pure anima is complete. She is no longer just woman but the archetypal image of all women. So extensive is the projection that he ascribes to her almost supernatural powers and insights.

MARIA

Maria remains undeveloped as a character because she functions as a specific type rather than as an autonomous individual. Her role in the novel is to teach Harry the art of living and lovemaking without feelings of guilt. This is an important factor in the balancing of Harry's character because he had always denied that part of his personality. Since Maria experiences life with naivete and innocence, she is the best of all possible teachers. She is a thoughtless butterfly who will live out her brief youth pursuing the most fleeting pleasure. For her, the real world consists of pleasure resorts, night clubs, and jazz bars. She is a master at extracting the utmost delight from the senses with which she is endowed. Her love and enthusiasm for popular songs as well as her childlike emotional response to a new dish or a little present not only teach Harry a great lesson in aesthetics but force him to reexamine his whole carefully constructed system. He marvels that her feelings are no less profound and exalted than his when he listens to a Mozart sonata. Harry finally understands that the secret of her intense happiness lies in her inability to view the world in terms of traditional morality. For her, the world is neither good nor bad - it simply is. This enables her to undergo the entire scale of human experience. Since her values are not absolute, she can enjoy lovemaking without being in love and can be the lover of many men at the same time. Finally, she teaches Harry that the enjoyment of life is heightened by not reflecting on the motivation and by not analyzing each sensation. In short, Maria, like the bourgeois narrator, lives in almost total harmony with herself and with the world. Unlike him, her happiness is not the dividend of self-discipline, the suppression of natural impulses, and the work syndrome, but her freedom from these values.

Of course, Hesse's presentation of Maria and her naive approach to life must not be regarded as a call for a return to innocence or as the panacea to our problems. Although a certain amount of bliss may be found in ignorance, there are many serious disadvantages. Such people as Maria and her friends fall easy prey to unscrupulous demagogues.

Furthermore, society's strength, progress, and humane values, not to mention the fine arts, do not emanate from this layer of society but from such men as Harry. The sole function of this **episode** is to help Harry bring his life into harmony by showing him that he is capable of both participating in that life and enjoying it.

PABLO

Like the other protagonists, Pablo functions on two levels. Perceived on the level of middle-class morality, he appears as a jaded hedonist whose interests are restricted to such delights as love orgies for three, psychedelic drugs, and other depravities. One immediately forms the picture of a slow-witted, prettified dandy who spends his time between orgies and trips indulging his bad taste in music and loud clothes, fiddling with his gaudy rings, and grinding out fatuities like: "You are so very unhappy.... Try a mild pipe of opium." His vacuous smile, vacant eyes, and monosyllabic small talk are not characteristics usually associated with intellectual agility. Furthermore, it develops that even his renowned proficiency in several languages is restricted to a few harmless phrases in each.

Yet as the novel progresses, it becomes apparent that his shallowness is deceptive. Harry lags far behind the reader in seeing that although Pablo is uneducated, he possesses extraordinary intuitive wisdom. The secret of Pablo's serenity is that he understands that if we are to live peacefully in the world, we must accept it as it is and not expect to find an ultimate unity beyond or within life. Since he knows that existence is meaningless, it follows that every individual is free to create his own personal meaning. The realization that the ultimate source of values is man himself allows Pablo to laugh at all efforts to categorize values or men. He cannot argue the merits of Mozart and jazz because for him both have the same essential quality since they are manifestations of the same phenomenon.

Pablo has injected meaning into his existence through his music. When performing, his face loses its trancelike immobility and radiates an almost sublime ecstasy. Since jazz allows the musician to create while playing, Pablo participates in the same creative process as Mozart and Bach. While his creations may be less refined, his sense of fulfillment and achievement are no less intense and have given him peace of mind. Serenity, inner harmony, and intuitive wisdom as well as creativity are all qualities that Harry associates with the Immortals. His double perception, therefore, elevates Pablo to the same rank as Goethe and Mozart.

Pablo is genuinely compassionate and is as concerned about Harry's mental health as he is about Agostino's physical illness. Although he may not entirely understand that Harry in the Magic Theater looks upon him as the Magus archetype, he is more than willing to assume the role of leader. Appreciating the power of suggestion when under the influence of drugs and knowing the source of Harry's problems, he is able to break down his friend's psychological defenses and show him what he must do to live a meaningful life.

It would, however, be wrong to view Pablo as Harry does. He is neither an Immortal nor an omniscient, archetypal wise man. Although he resembles them in many ways, it is on a much lower level than Harry portrays them.

CHRONOLOGICAL TABLE OF HESSE'S MAIN WORKS

....

1899 An Hour Beyond Midnight

1901 Hermann Lauscher

1904 Peter Camenzind

1906 Beneath the Wheel

1910 Gertrude

1914 Rosshalde

1915 Knulp

1919 Demian, "Zarathustra's Return", *In Sight of Chaos*, "Klein and Wagner"

1920 Klingsor's Last Summer

1922 Siddhartha

1925 Kurgast

1927 Steppenwolf

1930 Narziss and Goldmund

1932 The Journey to the East

1943 The Glass Bead Game

1951 Late Prose, Letters

STEPPENWOLF

ESSAY QUESTIONS AND ANSWERS

Question: What is the role of humor in *Steppenwolf*?

Answer: Humor provides peace of mind and assures productivity for that class of men who long to break free of their attachment to the bourgeois but are unable to do so. It is the only positive alternative to their present self-destructive condition. Despising the bourgeois yet belonging to it, their alienation has destroyed any possibility of human companionship and has reduced their lives to misery and suffering. They are enraged by the banality of the middle-class way of life, infuriated by the degradation of the arts in the modern age, and grieved at the trivialization of the soul through technology. The Treatise says that the world afflicts men like Harry because they have committed the error of making value judgments. Of course, one cannot make value judgments until he has first categorized the world into an arbitrary system of right and wrong. This is the real source of maladjustment. Inner tranquility and self-contempt is the price one pays for measuring everything according to a rigid, immutable standard. In a way, one becomes the victim of his values.

The Treatise points out that we may escape from this vicious circle and live serenely in the world free of its many irritations by learning the secret of humor. Since humor has something of the bourgeois in it, though inaccessible to the true bourgeois, a person can learn its power without first freeing himself from that class. Humor is defined as a state of mind approaching, but not including, that of the Immortals. It signifies above all the refusal, even the incapacity, to judge the world by one's personal values. Moreover, humor reconciles and affirms all polarities, contradictions, and discordant aspects of life. Not only can one then reconcile such opposites as saint, sinner, and bourgeois but also jazz, Mozart, and call girls. Furthermore, humor enables its master to view life in a detached way, to live in the world without being a part of it, and to be immune to the irritations and absurdities of reality. In other words, a person who possesses humor understands that the world must be accepted at face value. It is neither good nor bad; it merely is. Recognizing this, he will see that it is false to view the world in terms of antithetical polarities and that opposites have been created in a vain effort to organize the world into a coherent, comprehensible order.

In the Magic Theater it is pointed out that in every truth the opposite is equally true. In fact, it is more than likely that the value of one truth lies in its identity with its opposite. Once the individual has comprehended these things through humor, he will be free of the love-hate relationship to the bourgeois that engenders so much suffering. Most importantly, since his vitality would no longer be sapped at its roots, his life would be more productive.

To learn humor, however, one must first come to terms with the discordant elements within his own Self. Thus the chief purpose of the Magic Theater is to lead Harry into his unconscious so that he may confront and accept what he finds there. He will then be able to laugh both at himself and at the world. Mozart aids Harry by giving him a magic mirror which, when activated by laughter, shatters the unified personality into its component parts. Each can then be examined individually. And again near the end of the novel, Mozart demonstrates to him exactly how he must act by dramatizing the problem with the radio broadcast of Handel's concerto. Behind the instrument's enraging distortions, the careful listener can nevertheless discern the original spirit of the music. If one responds to the world in a like manner, he can laugh at life's inconsistencies and paradoxes while honoring that which is beautiful and sublime.

Laughter becomes symbol during the dream interview with Goethe when he tells Harry that the Immortals do not like things to be taken seriously, least of all themselves. They prefer a good joke instead. As a young man, he too took things seriously and longed for eternity, but he soon realized that it was wrong to do so. It is much better to laugh. From Goethe, Harry hears in the laughter everything he longs and strives for. It is significant that laughter is always described by such words as star-bright, metallic, eerie, and frigid. It is appropriate that the laughter of the Immortals should be described in terms denoting cold because that is also the characteristic we most frequently associate with indifference and non-involvement: precisely the attitude that both the Treatise and Mozart urge Harry to acquire.

Question: How can the bourgeois, the Immortal, and the Steppenwolf be compared?

Answer: The fundamental difference between these three kinds of men lies in their world view. The bourgeois conceives the universe in a mechanistic way, metaphorically as a perfectly running machine, and he regards himself as an integral part of that machine. Since the universe is perfect, change is negative. He believes that this is the best of all possible worlds and that bourgeois society is the best of all possible societies. Because they judge not only things but also one another according to how well they fit, they seek above all to organize their own lives in a way that will insure the smooth function of society. Since society loses the talents and gifts of the men who prefer to be consumed by the inner fire of total commitment, the bourgeois strives to preserve a balance between the countless extremes of which human nature is capable. Of course, walking the middle of the road assures tranquility of mind and preserves the identity, but comfort and security can be attained only at the sacrifice of change, growth, and liberty. His values are changelessness, uniformity, conformity, and the group. This is the irreconcilable difference between the bourgeois and the Immortal. It is nothing less than a conflict between world views.

The Immortals, on the other hand, conceive the universe organically, metaphorically as a tree. That is, the universe - and society - is not an immutable something that has been set running for all time. It is in an eternal state of becoming, or growing. The universe is alive. Therefore, the values held in highest esteem are growth, change, and creation. Furthermore, since something that grows cannot be perfect, imperfection is no longer a negative value but a positive one. If the world is viewed in this way, the necessity of accepting the world at face value is obvious.

The chief characteristic of Hesse's Immortals is their ability to deny nothing, understand and affirm everything - i.e., everything except the bourgeois. In spite of their willingness to accept the world as it is, the Immortals cannot affirm that tepid middle ground between the extremes to which the individual may commit himself. For the Immortals, life devoid of intensity is anathema. Viewing the world as imperfect and human life as meaningless, they accept this condition as an opportunity to create their own meaning. So they break away from society and plunge into the untrammeled regions of total commitment. It must be pointed out that the object of the first importance is the ecstasy derived from devoting the whole of one's being to a single object. It matters little what one pursues. As the Treatise suggests, it may be the spiritual life of the saint or the profligate's corruption of the flesh. It could just as well be a commitment to the arts as Mozart and Goethe were committed, or to the improvement of the social conditions as the revolutionary. To be sure, intensity of feeling means a certain loss of identity and even involves being captive to one's excesses. But sometimes nothing succeeds like excess. Here the basic difference between the bourgeois and the Immortal stands out most clearly. The bourgeois regards the Self as his most precious possession and strives to preserve it at all costs. The Immortal looks upon the Self and the entire personality as the instrument by which he may grasp the unconditional.

The Steppenwolf, by contrast, wanders somewhere between the two, sharing elements of both but belonging to neither. He longs to make the leap into the unconditional but is unable to do so because he denies part of his personality. He cannot affirm the organic conception of the universe because that requires accepting things as they are. Neither can he identify with the bourgeois' mechanistic view because its values are perfection, changelessness, and conformity. Consequently, he has evolved a dualistic interpretation of the universe. This is best illustrated by the way he has divided his own personality into man and wolf. To the man side he assigns everything that is beautiful, noble, and sublime, while to the wolf side he assigns everything savage, raw, and cruel.

Harry's dualistic view pervades every aspect of his thinking. With frightening consistency he divides the world into irreconcilable, warring polarities. For him, music resembles either the steam from raw meat or the striding of gods, love is either tragic longing or coarse passion, and human values are either flesh or spirit. Harry pays a high price for his world view. His productivity is crippled, his personality poisoned, and his striving rendered useless.

Question: How is the Magic Theater connected to the rest of the novel?

Answer: A comparison of the Magic Theater with the rest of the book reveals the careful construction of the novel, for each event of the theater both repeats a **theme** introduced elsewhere and enables Harry to experience as reality the knowledge he had gained during the past four weeks. Fifteen sideshows are mentioned, among them suicide, humor, solitude, love, metamorphoses, the decline of Western civilization. Whether Harry enters these rooms or not, each implies the resolution of that specific problem.

Harry's first experience recapitulates the Treatise's discourse on the multifarious nature of the personality. The Treatise says that it is wrong to view the Self as consisting of only one or two parts when in fact it is made up of thousands. Harry grasps the lesson when he looks into the magic mirror and watches his personality break into some of its segments. He sees himself simultaneously as an old man, young man, humanitarian, lover, and many others. Now that he recognizes the true nature of his personality, he may begin the descent into the unconscious.

The following scene recalls **episodes** from his friendship with Pablo and Maria. A youth and a handsome young man spring out of the mirror. While the first dashes down the hallway and hurls himself into the slot that promises the love of all girls, the other goes off with Pablo. We remember that Pablo and Maria are proficient in lovemaking with both sexes and that a love orgy for three was once suggested which Harry indignantly refused. Later, when Harry enters the same room into which the youth had disappeared, he enjoys there the love of all the women he ever knew. Thus, the resolution of polarity in physical love is indicated.

The Great Automobile Hunt deflates Harry's pacifism and dramatizes the Treatise's claim that the individual must recognize his potential for committing and enjoying every human act from the most brutal to the most noble. Sitting on a platform erected in the branches of a tree and shooting passing motorists, Harry, the renowned pacifist, discovers that he is not only able to kill and enjoy war but that it is great sport.

Harry experiences in the booth marked Guidance In Constructing The Personality an idea first introduced in the Treatise. The prevailing view maintains that the parts of the personality are arranged in an immutable series that form a clearly detached and fixed unit. This interpretation is founded on a false analogy. Since the body is an indivisible entity that can function only as a unit, it follows that since the personality is a resident of the body, it too is a unit. Even though the Treatise proclaims the multiplicity of the personality, Harry is not willing to accept it. His antipathy, however, is dispelled by the chessplayer.

When the magic mirror breaks Harry's personality into pieces, Pablo arranges them on the board for a game. The pieces form liaisons, factions, groups, and go about the business of living. Several times Pablo rearranges the pieces in no definite order and each time the game, although related, is different.

Finally, one of the chief **metaphors** of the novel is externalized when the Treatise's abstractions on the nature of humor are made real. We recall that Harry is told to stop taking himself seriously and learn the power of humor if he wants to live in harmony with himself and the world. This theme is developed extensively in the **episode** following the murder of Hermine's image. Learn what to take seriously, says Pablo, and laugh at all the rest. Only the spirit behind the phenomena merits our honor, not its external manifestation.

ANNOTATED BIBLIOGRAPHY

Abood, Edward. "Jung's Concept of Individuation in Hesse's *Steppenwolf*," *Southern Humanities Review*, Vol. 3 (1969), 1-13. Analyzes the novel in terms of Jungian psychology.

Boulby, Mark. *Hermann Hesse: His Mind and Art*. Ithaca, New York, 1967. Thorough and penetrating analysis of Hesse's works; a standard work on the subject.

Brunner, John W. "The Natur-Geist Polarity in Hermann Hesse," *Helen Adolf Festschrift*, New York (1968), pp. 268-284. Examines Hesse's presentation of the conflict between the natural and spiritual impulses in man and his efforts to resolve the polarity.

Cohn, Dorrit. "Narration of Consciousness in *Der Steppenwolf*," *Germanic Review*, Vol. 44 (1969), 121-131. Treats the style of the novel with particular attention to the way the protagonist's consciousness is rendered.

Colby, Thomas E. "The Impenitent Prodigal: Hermann Hesse's Hero," *German Quarterly*, Vol. 40 (1967), 14-23. Examines the Prodigal Son motif in Hesse's works.

Flaxman, Seymour. "*Der Steppenwolf*: Hesse's Portrait of the Intellectual," *Modern Language Quarterly*, Vol. 15 (1954), 349-358. Textual analysis.

Freedman, Ralph. *The Lyrical Novel*. Princeton, 1963. Treats *Steppenwolf* along with Andre Gide and Virginia Woolf. Excellent criticism.

Heller, Peter. "The Writer in Conflict with his Age: A Study in the Ideology of Hermann Hesse," *Monatshefte*, Vol. 46 (1954), 137-147. Establishes Hesse's ideological position to society.

Hughes, Kenneth. "Hesse's Use of Gilgamesh-Motifs in the Humanization of Siddhartha and Harry Haller," *Seminar*, Vol. 5 (1969), 129-140. Examines the role of woman in elevating Hesse's heroes to a higher level of perception.

Mileck, Joseph. *Hermann Hesse and His Critics*. Chapel Hill, N.C., 1958. Bibliography through 1955. Complete discussion of Hesse criticism. Scholarly, thorough, and essential.

Norton, Roger C. "Hermann Hesse's Criticism of Technology," *Germanic Review*, Vol. 43 (1968), 267-273. Defines Hesse's attitude to technological progress.

Rose, Ernst. *Faith from the Abyss*. New York, 1956. Textual analysis.

Schmid, Hans R. *Hermann Hesse*. Leipzig, 1928. Analyzes Hesse's work in terms of Jungian and Freudian psychology. Very good, although he sometimes forces the point.

Schmid, Max. *Hermann Hesse: Weg und Wandlung*. Zurich, 1947. **Metaphysical** treatment of Hesse's works from *Demian* to *The Glass Bead Game*.

Schwarz, Egon. "Zur Erklärung von Hesses *Steppenwolf*," *Monatshefte*, Vol. 63 (1961), 191-198. Textual analysis and compares Hesse's novel and Goethe's *Wilhelm Meister's Apprenticeship*.

Waibler, Helmut. *Hermann Hesse: Eine Bibliographie*. Bern and Munich, 1962. Excellent bibliography through 1961.

Ziolkowski, Theodore. "Hermann Hesse's Chiliastic Vision," *Monatshefte*, Vol. 53 (1964), 199-210. Outlines the triadic structure of human development (innocence-guilt-redemption) in Hesse's work.

___. *The Novels of Hermann Hesse*. Princeton, 1965. Immensely readable. The most authoritative criticism to date. Penetrating structural analysis of the prose work, much background material. Essential for a thorough understanding of Hesse. Available in paperback.

___. "Saint Hesse Among the Hippies," *American-German Review*, Vol. 35 (1969), 19-23. Explains the reasons for Hesse's popularity in this country. Whatever Ziolkowski writes is worthwhile.

www.ingramcontent.com/pod-product-compliance
Lightning Source LLC
LaVergne TN
LVHW011731060526
838200LV00051B/3137